The Darien Jungle
Shakedown Cruise

The Darien Jungle Shakedown Cruise

By

C. Buck Weimer

ISBN: **978-0-615-25185-1**

Library of Congress Control Number: **To be determined.**

Dedication

I lovingly dedicate this book to my wife, Arlene, the greatest partner I could ever have hoped for; to my three wonderful sons, Jonathan, Matthew, and Adam, who taught me so much; and to my unseen friends (for good and proper personal reasons) for their help along the way.

I would like to thank those who have greatly helped me during the editing process: Arlene Weimer, Lynn Chapman, Kelly Phillips, Jo Ann Wiedman, Maralyn Oestrich, and the special work of Aurora Hill.

Author's Note

T he manuscript for this book was originally written in 1967. And though attempts were made, it remained unpublished gathering dust in a cardboard box. Over the years, I told snippets of the adventure to aghast family members and unbelieving friends, but never the whole story.

As my three boys grew into manhood, they became more persistent in their encouragement for me to take advantage of the internet method of publishing a book; as a family legacy at a minimum. When my wife joined the chorus I knew it was time.

The problem for me was: how to rewrite something written so long ago?

In the original manuscript, I wrote in the *past* tense, and decided to have it printed in the font size and style you are now reading. Also in the original writing, I occasionally imbedded small portions of the fading and deteriorating journal notes into the manuscript. This rambling indicated what I was thinking and doing *at the moment* while in the jungle. Printed for this book it is in ***bold and italicized***.

Slowly I began the arduous process of transferring the old manuscript from the dried paper pages, typed on an old Underwood manual typewriter, into my computer hard-drive. In the process, a strong need naturally arose within me to share with the reader some reflections of where I am *now*. This thought process is printed here *underlined and italicized*, to separate the present from the past. Forty years of living after the completion of the original manuscript gave birth to a host of new perspectives.

By visually separating the past from the present, the hope is to provide the reader with a more clear understanding and allow for a more complete sharing of the total, sometimes inexplicable, experience. A map of the entire trip is on page 12, and a map of the trek through the Darien Jungle is on page 194.

Contents

Chapter 1

My left boot became momentarily stuck in a well-anchored root.

Tripping, I stumbled forward in a vain attempt to avoid falling. But I fell with a grunt and landed face-first in the dirt near the hilltop.

I just laid there for a while, too exhausted to get up. Salty sweat streamed down my forehead burning my eyes and blurring my vision. I could barely lift my head or move my hands. I peered at the ground only inches away trying to focus and make the dizzy spots go away. My onrushing breath scattered flaky specks of dust and tiny pieces of bark onto my hands spread before me. I felt pieces of dirt going deeper and deeper down my moist throat with each gasp.

A community of ants, ticks and sundry insects scurried around in chaos, under and over the obstacles in their environment in search of each other. I almost snickered at the comparison. Were we just like them or were they just like us? At that moment I felt as if I were fodder for the jungle; food for its evolutionary growth. I was about to become one with the jungle.

My death would not make the headlines in any newspaper; if anyone were unfortunate enough to find my body before it was fully consumed by the living earth. And, except for relatives and a few friends, I would be forgotten. It would be just another death in the forbidden jungle; just another lost soul into the unknown.

Tears welled in my eyes and I began to weep. I was despondent and believed I was about to die. My body seemed unable to carry me. It would have been so easy to just die there, to give up.

Ha, some shakedown cruise.

* * * * *

At least once for every person there occurs a catalytic event drastically changing the course of his life. This is a story about just such an experience.

I spent thirty-one days walking, riding, and swimming through nearly two hundred miles of the Darien Jungle in Panama while attempting to complete an overland motorcycle trip from North America to South America - alone.

It was a wildly conceived, crudely executed scheme from the very beginning, and by all the laws of nature, logic of mind, and intuition should never have been started, much less completed. Nonetheless, I did it, and it proved to be a great adventure in my quest to understand ultimate questions and what it is like to be a person and a man.

Outwardly, I fit into the description of the average person in America; knew it, and felt stifled by it. I often referred to myself as "Mr. In-between", a middle child between a younger brother and older sister, growing up in an era between swing music and rock n' roll, Beatniks and Hippies, Kerouac and Hemmingway, straddling the line between conformity and non-conformity. I liked Bogart, but loved James Dean. But it was Jack Kerouac's "On the Road" and his glistening characters compelled to experience the world on their own terms that was the most influential.

Kay Starr's transition song "Rock and Roll Waltz" was one of my favorites.

Inwardly, I felt awkward with myself and was, mentally and morally, completely without discipline. These characteristics when combined with being a natural risk-taker have the potential for disastrous consequences.

However, it was really the fear of stagnation and the dread of monotony that ultimately propelled me to undertake this journey and move me into action. I wanted to experience a new adventure, exceed my boundaries, and do something unique, something nobody had ever done before.

Inadvertently, the Darien Jungle became the stage whereupon more than an adventure of a lifetime was enacted.

Few people know about this jungle and even fewer people care to know about it. And, if you were to drive a vehicle from anywhere in North America and head south through Mexico and continue through Central America until you reached the country of Panama, you would eventually run out of highway and smack into an unimagined green thickness of trees and vegetation, the Darien Jungle.

Sometimes known as the Isthmus of Panama, or the Darien Gap, it begins where the Pan American Highway ends, and continues its way to the foothills of the towering Andes Mountains in Colombia. Its formidable forest is the last section of the ever-changing landscape along the routes of the Alcan and Pan American highways that stretch down the entire Western Hemisphere (19,000 miles - 30,600 km). It has remained impenetrable to the bulldozer from northern Alaska to the southern tip of Chile, and remains a stumbling block to the advancement of modern civilization.

Since then, I have greatly altered my views on the natural environment – mother earth. The Darien Jungle currently represents, perhaps, the second most important ecological area in the Americas – outside the Amazon basin – and one of the top ten in the world. It simply must be preserved! Building a road through this jungle would completely destroy what is left. At the time of my journey, it was approximately 300 miles(483 kilometers) from the beginning to the border of Colombia. The most recent reports show an estimated 93 miles (150 kilometers) to the border.

As a land mass, the Darien Jungle is rather meek by most standards: less than twenty air-miles wide at the narrowest point and nearly seventy-five air-miles long when measured as the crow flies. There is a small range of low level mountains stretching down the length of the jungle like the vertebrae of a prehistoric animal. The actual length of the Gap in miles is not positively known, for it has never been rightfully surveyed, but best-guess estimate is a few clicks less than two hundred miles.

Descriptively however, it represents a jungle in the classic sense with its rugged terrain, dense foliage, wild birds and animals, bare-skinned Indians, over a hundred inches of rain per season, and millions upon millions of insects of every size and variety. It has the mystic power to capture your mind with its halting and mesmerizing beauty, while stimulating your most primordial imagination.

At the time, I was traveling alone on a Honda 150cc motorcycle and riding on the crest of a planned overland trip from California to somewhere (anywhere) in South America, and the momentum had just carried me from Los Angeles to Panama City. Of course, I was warned repeatedly by everyone I spoke to in Panama that the only possible way to get into South America was to ferry my Honda by boat around the Darien Jungle and into Buenaventura, Colombia, near Cali. Once there, the Pan American highway would resume. However, being a hard-headed person with a one-track mind, I refused to be treated like a common tourist after having traveled overland so far, and getting so close, only to submit to a ride on a ferry boat. I decided to drive straight into the jungle on the motorcycle and hoped to make history by becoming the first person to drive a motorcycle from North America to South America entirely overland.

Alas, the jungle quickly took its toll !

I soon found myself fighting through unfamiliar and hostile terrain with little knowledge of survival skills, a machete for protection, a compass to guide me, and a very poor map from which to guess my position. The scales between life and death often quivered in a delicate balance; tilted only by shear determination. My will exceeded my skills. Eventually I became one of only a handful of men to traverse the entire length of the Darien Jungle and write about it. By so doing, I discovered more about the world, the people in it, and especially about myself, than if I had lived a hundred years in any urban or suburban society of the modern world.

Often I was pushed to the farthest extent of my physical endurance, carried to the length, depth, and breadth of every feeling that could possibly be evoked from the crevices of my being. But more importantly, I had a chance to observe myself as an entity separated from almost all human and social influences, away from the pop bottles, automobiles, and the big cities. For the first time I had an opportunity to observe how heredity and the environment contrive to make a human being.

This was my shakedown cruise, the first time I cast off unassisted on a new adventure. Always, in the past, when seeking new experiences or going off to different terrain I had been with at least one other person – sometimes two, three, or more. Now it was time to go solo.

*   *   *   *   *

The story began in North Hollywood, a suburb of Los Angeles, California in1964 long before I knew the Darien Jungle existed. I was twenty-five years old, and had recently returned to the United States after being discharged from the U.S. Military on Okinawa and crewing on a thirty-foot trimaran sailboat in the

Japanese Islands. I realized I was nearing the age when most people, after finishing high school, serving in the military, and sowing a few wild oats, would be ready to settle down to the usual toils of everyday living.

But this was not possible for me!

I felt an almost desperate urgency to get out and do things "before it was too late". I shunned responsibility and only owned one possession, a car.

And what a beauty it was – a 1955 MG, convertible, 1500 series, a red body with black fenders, spoke wheels and all!

I was unmarried, had no family living in California, and was primed for adventure. I lived in North Hollywood with the Hinkle family, for whose generosity, forgiving tolerance, and moral guidance I will forever be grateful. Their son Bill and I were in the paratroopers together and crewed on the same sailboat.

So I found myself working for a small Los Angeles Manufacturer, Bob Mitchell Designs, as a silk-screen printer eating peanut-butter sandwiches and saving as much money as possible. However, I had no particular goal or place in the world I wanted to visit – just a strong desire to go to a place I had never been previously, and to do something I had never done before.

I can still remember when I finally made the great decision. I was sitting at home in my single, ill-lit room, ruminating about my life, while trying to ward off the nervousness of wanting to travel, travel, and travel. I had managed to save five hundred dollars and wanted to go as far and stay as long as my money would permit. I had already been to the Orient, and Europe seemed a long way away and not very exciting.

Suddenly, I was struck with the idea of going to South America. I'd often heard and read a lot about its romanticism and excitement, and the name had always sounded strange and exotic.

In my excitement, I wanted to leave that very minute. My mind raced with a thousand visions, and I kept repeating: "I'm going to South America! I'm going to South America!" Suddenly, I felt so relieved now that I had some direction and knew where I was going. My mind stayed in a state of excitement even as I switched off the bedroom light and tried to force myself to sleep.

The next morning the realities of my decision confronted me with the sobering question of just exactly how I was going to travel the long and certainly dusty road to South America. The relief I experienced the night before soon gave way to anxiety. I didn't want to walk or hitchhike the many thousands of miles to South America. Both took too long. Financially, flying was out of the question. The only real choice left was to drive into South America. However, I didn't want the responsibilities of the MG, or any other automobile for such a long period of time.

Thus, a motorcycle seemed to be the only mode of transportation which could fit all my needs: small investment, excellent gas mileage, little maintenance, and most important, it would permit me an almost unlimited maneuverability and flexibility in travel.

There was only one minor problem: I had never driven a motorcycle before!

However, I refused to allow my dream of driving to South America on a motorcycle be forestalled because of a small detail like my driving skills – or lack thereof.

Within two weeks immediately following my all-important decision, I was actually ready to leave Los Angeles and head south. I never bothered to clutter my mind with such trivia as road conditions along the Pan American route, weather conditions in the tropical regions, nor political or economic situations of the many countries about to be visited.

I traded the snazzy MG sports car for a 1964 Honda 150cc motor-cycle. It was an even trade, plus $200 the buyer, a biker friend, still owed me.

Probably the poorest financial deal of my life!

This Honda was just the perfect size for my five foot eight inch, one hundred and fifty pound frame.

I left my job, obtained a new passport and bought the equipment I felt would be needed for the journey.

The motorcycle was a new experience, and quickly captured my imagination. I spent hours each day learning how to ride – shifting gears, making sharp turns, and balancing the motorcycle on irregular terrain. The engine ran like a finely tuned watch. It was easily prepared and equipped for the long ride: a chrome luggage-rack was bolted onto the top of the rear fender and acted as an extension of the seat, a set of black saddle-bags were strapped firmly on each side of the rear fender, a rubberized water-proof bag contained extra clothing, and a sleeping bag was tied to the luggage rack. Money, passport, and all personal belongings were placed inside the saddle-bags in a plastic container.

Once all the gear was readied and the Honda checked by a mechanic, the only decision needing to be made was the date of departure; a fact that, when given enough leeway, would easily lead to procrastination.

A major character flaw.

The 1964 Christmas season was approaching and I felt it necessary to leave the country before the onslaught of all the partying, the gift buying, and other obligations connected with it. Then there would be the New Years holiday, and my birthday following soon after – January 15th. If I didn't leave California before Christmas, I might not get away before early spring – if at all.

With this in mind, I decided all systems were a "GO" and to head for the Mexican border on the twentieth of December; leaving behind several less-than intimate female relationships.

*   *   *   *   *

It was raining hard on the Sunday of my departure.

Patiently I waited for the downpour to stop, but it persisted. I knew I had to be true to my pledged word to leave on the twentieth as planned. Mounting the wet cushioned seat of the Honda, I started the engine and said my last few words to the Hinkle family, and especially to son Bill; my Dean Moriarty. In my cheap plastic rain-suit, white crash helmet, and black motorcycle boots I felt like an astronaut preparing for a blast-off. With a twinge of bravado, I waved goodbye to the concerned faces and roared shakily into the pelting rain; heading south.

*   *   *   *   *

I lost my way three times while trying to unravel the mystery of the Los Angeles freeway system. A highway patrolman stopped me and returned the license plate that had fallen off the Honda. My super-protective rain-suit had been torn to shreds from the constant flapping in the wind from the fifty mile-an-hour driving. The words of the Beatles' song "Can't Buy Me Love" and thoughts of Cuba, Cassius Clay, Jack Ruby, Lyndon Johnson, and Martin Luther King Jr. alternated between hope and despair inside my head.

Ten hours and two hundred miles later I arrived at the Salton Sea – at the southeastern tip of California; a long way from Nogales, Arizona where I hoped to cross into Mexico. To make matters worse every muscle and bone in my body ached, and I had a splitting headache.

From a distance, it looked like a sandy beach around the Salton. Turns out, it is actually zillions of barnacles and dead fish bones. Foam and algae is everywhere with the strong smell of sulfur constant. It looks almost like a moonscape. The stars, and the Milky Way, are so overwhelmingly bright and beautiful tonight. Looking up seems to help my headache. Wow! What a treat! There's a shooting star; another one. Sleepy now. I'd always identified with Sal Paradise. Maybe this is my chance to be Dean.

My only consolation that first night in the sleeping bag was in knowing that tomorrow I would be *somewhere* in Mexico; far into the first leg of my journey to South America.

The next morning I arose shortly after it was light and began forming a series of habits that were to carry me through the entire trip to Panama City: always awakening at least thirty minutes before sunrise, dress, roll up the sleeping bag, drink some fluids, and start the Honda to warm the engine. I would drive all day long stopping only for fuel and occasionally for something to eat, and then drive for several hours into the darkness of each night. My last task for the day was to find a lonely spot several hundred yards off to either side of the highway where I would sleep for the night in order to save money.

For the first week or so I drove like a madman - a man possessed – for twelve and sometimes fourteen hours each day. I went down the road like a race horse wearing blinders. I looked straight ahead without caring what was on either side of the road. There was a relentless drive within me to keep moving; to go forward, no matter what. My stomach muscles felt as though they were tied in knots, and I usually suffered from a headache due to the excitement, hunger pains, and thirst. Even the foreign landscape of Mexico was only a minor distraction from the growing obsession of reaching South America.

Nogales was sensory paradise, with dusty streets, a lot of loud music, the smell of distinctive food everywhere, and barking dogs on every corner. It was very different, and I loved it!

Hot food, cold beer, and lots of friendly people. This is the life for me!

The ride from Nogales to the city of Mazatlan seemed never-ending. All I can remember about it was the many hours spent "in the saddle" – riding. Fortunately that afforded me the opportunity to gain the necessary experience needed to handle the motorcycle with the skills and dexterity required on the later unfamiliar and more difficult roads. I would practice quick mounts and dismounts, starting and stopping, and test my stability at extremely slow speeds and again at extremely high speeds. And, because the road to Mazatlan was lightly traveled, I practiced a great deal of "trick-riding". My favorite ride was to zigzag the Honda between the monotonous miles of broken white lines in the center of the roads. The real hazards to driving, however, were the meandering cows that appeared to believe the highways were made exclusively for them.

I felt god-like as the motorcycle obeyed my every command and followed even the slightest movement of my body. The choice was mine: go left, go right, go forward, faster or slower.

This freedom is exhilarating and addictive.

My fondest memories of that first fifteen hundred miles into Mexico were the beautiful sensations I felt each evening while riding the Honda into the warm, dusty, sundown. I would hurry; almost scurry to the top of the next rolling hill trying to catch one quicker glimpse of the huge, flaming sun before it passed out of sight. It seemed as if I was literally chasing after the sunsets.

One of my lasting memories of this part of the journey happened late one day as the sun was in the low part of the afternoon sky. I had been driving behind an overloaded truck for what seemed like forever – catching the back draft and using almost no gasoline. Out of sheer madness, I pulled up close enough to the back of the steady-moving truck and grabbed onto the tailgate and held on as the truck towed me along at fifty miles an hour for as many miles as the strength of my grip would allow.

GENERAL ROUTE
The Darien Jungle Shakedown Cruise

It was crazy, I know, but indicative of my level of risk-taking.

Finally, I took a twenty-four hour break on the warm beaches of Mazatlan, Mexico. It was Christmas Day and I needed a rest on the dry sand in the brilliant tropical sun to rejuvenate my worn body and tired mind.

As I left Mazatlan on the twenty-sixth of December I decided to crisscross the southern half of Mexico. I had been following the Pan American Highway along the western coast of Mexico and wanted to detour slightly from this route for the sake of sight-seeing while hoping at the same time to relieve some of my pent-up anxiety about getting to South America.

I drove to Guadalajara and then to Mexico City, and decided to continue eastward to the fabled seaport city of Vera Cruz, on the Atlantic side of the Mexican continent.

As it turned out, it was a near-fatal decision.

I left Mexico City on a warm, bright, morning as the new year of 1965 began and assumed there would be no difficulty driving the 300 miles to Vera Cruz. As the late afternoon sun began to set, the road began a gradual incline and the weather cooled, requiring me to take a jacket out of the saddle bags. After an hour of continuous uphill driving it began to rain; and then *snow* started falling. I couldn't believe it! *Snow* at this southern latitude – 19 degrees North!

I was terminally naïve. To drive from Mexico City to Vera Cruz necessitated going over or around Mt. Orizaba! At 18,695 feet (5,636 meters) it is the 3rd highest mountain peak in North America and part of the Trans-Mexican volcanic belt – Eje Volcanicao Transversal. Native Indians call it "White Mountain".

The Honda was slipping and sliding all over the road. Because of the holidays and weather conditions I saw no other vehicles in either direction. The snow got deeper and deeper. There were no houses or building, no lights – nothing. I was afraid to stop for fear of not being able to start again.

In the distance, I thought I could see a small light.

As I drove still higher the light became larger and brighter. Finally I saw a building and parked the Honda beside the steps to the doorway. It was an adobe church and the light was from burning candles.

Inside it was completely empty of humans. And, despite the fact that there was no heating system, it felt warm and cozy. I slept the night on a wood bench; happy to be safe from the cold, wind, and snow.

In retrospect, this was my first conscious spiritual experience, even though I didn't recognize it as such at the time. Finding that candle-lit church near the top of the road in the white night did more than just save my physical life.

The next morning the sky was clear, and the drive down the mountain was quick and uneventful – despite the initial slick conditions.

Vera Cruz was warm and friendly, and I loved it. But I couldn't stay for more than two days before this inner drive forced me to continue south along the eastern coast.

The journey south was jammed with many personal vignettes. To tell them all, even some of the short ones, would be a great distraction.

This one, however, is worth a short diversion.

As I pulled into a gas station in the small town of Santiago Tuxtla, a friendly voice greeted me, in English, from across the road. The voice was that of a Mexican man in his fifties, and he identified himself as Dr. Ricardo Alvarez. He invited me to rest for a while in his home. The sign on the doorway indicated it was also his medical clinic. He was a very jovial man and said he learned English as a young man in the United States while working in Chicago as a driver for Al Capone; a real stretch of the imagination, but that's what he said. His wife did the cooking, usually frowned, and said very little.

As it turned out, I stayed in his home for several days. After a while, I began to notice most of his patients had a similar profile: young, well-dressed women wearing a lot of makeup. One night another English-speaking man from Santiago told me the purpose of Dr. Alvarez's "clinic". Apparently, the women patients were prostitutes from Mexico City and Dr. Alvarez would sew stitches in strategic locations of the vagina. These women would consequently make huge sums of money as a "virgin" prostitute, or even accept a marriage proposal from a naive man believing he had an untouched bride. On the wedding night, upon penetration, the stitches would tear causing the outside of the vagina to bleed.

Actually, this guy was way ahead of his time. Currently, there is a new procedure gaining prominence in the medical profession called "hymenoplasty" – a re-sewing of the hymen.

Dr. Alvarez also manipulated me into having tea in the family living room at the home of a young and beautiful *senorita* – alone. Big mistake! I quickly discovered that participating in this behavior was tantamount to being engaged to be married.

Needless to say, I quickly scampered out of Santiago Tuxtla as soon as possible and got back on the road of destiny.

Continuing south, the country of Mexico narrowed like the neck of a funnel making it easy to drive the dependable Honda over the short mountain range to the West coast; anticipating my return to the Pan American Highway.

*   *   *   *   *

Nearing Central America my earlier infatuation for the Honda had worn off and now became a full fledged love affair. Respect and pride for this mechanical device welled inside me, as it carried me over the seemingly endless miles of rolling macadam following my every command. Even the gear-shifting mistakes or the braking errors I made did little to hamper the bike's performance. I was able to maintain different riding positions for hours at a time, readily changing positions from sitting to standing (my favorite), to the prone. It was almost as if the bike had been custom made for me. And, during the entire tour of Mexico, I did no more to the engine than add oil and change the worn spark-plugs.

However, as I neared the border of Guatemala, I must admit to the first major riding mishap or "spill".

I was riding over a series of small mountains, small when compared to Mt. Orizaba, with very narrow and windy roads while crossing the Isthmus of Tehuantepec; in my effort to return to the Pan American Highway. I was trying to *avoid* the beauty of the sun-speckled countryside far below by keeping my eyes on the road directly in front of me. Near the top of one of the peaks, a small black convertible car came rushing down the mountain road toward me. In the car was a young man and two lovely *senoritas*. I couldn't restrain myself from staring at them – if only for a few short seconds. But a few seconds was all the time necessary for the Honda to steer itself off the paved road, down a shallow gully, and into the side of the rocky mountain.

I was quickly and rudely awakened from my fantasies, and, fortunately thrown clear of the falling motorcycle. The engine coughed and the wheels spun for a few moments before stopping. Once the numbness subsided I realized there was no apparent damage to my body. I was able to get the Honda upright and walked it back onto the paved road. The harrowing part of this accident was the place I drove off the road. Had I driven off the left side I would have fallen hundreds of feet down the sharp side of the mountain and into oblivion.

Once inside the borders of Central America the quick pace at which I traveled through the many countries became, to me, dazzling. Each day I would visit a different country. There was Guatemala, El Salvador, Honduras, Nicaragua, and then Costa Rica. With the exception of Costa Rica, I spent only a small amount of time in each capital city. But each country, each city, each section of the highway carried me closer to my coveted goal of South America. The roads were paved for a mile, then unpaved and rough for a mile; paved for a mile, unpaved and rough for a mile; on and on and on. The fair weather was better than I had expected, and of course the Honda 150cc was performing superbly. The "cruise" was working perfectly.

Then, as always happens when things are going too perfectly, everything came crashing down.

I was driving on the road leading into San Jose, Costa Rica when I sustained my most serious accident thus far. Once again I was staring at the girls. I was forced to jam on the brakes in the gravel near the side of the road while trying to over-correct my position. The Honda skidded for nearly a hundred feet down the road while I tried unsuccessfully to keep it upright. I ended up trying to maintain my own balance as I slid on my hands and knees.

The bike was badly damaged: the handle-bars were twisted, the gas-tank dented and scratched, and the spark plugs grossly misfired. But, I was lucky! I got away with only a few large, but minor brush burns. As I sputtered into San Jose I was overwhelmed with a premonition of worse things to come.

The physical damages to the bike and me were nothing compared to the shattering news I received after settling into a hotel room in downtown San Jose.

While at the Honda repair shop, I met three American bikers (motorcyclists) driving up the Pan American Highway from Panama on their way returning to the United States. First they informed me of the hazardous road conditions they encountered between San Jose and Panama City. Then they gave me the most crushing news of all: bluntly stating there was no road of any kind just south of Panama City. The road simply ended about thirty-five miles south-east of Panama City at a small town called Chepo. The Pan American Highway didn't resume again, they said, until somewhere in Colombia – nearly four hundred miles away.

The three men had driven their motorcycles (one a Honda 500, one Indian, and the other an incredible drive-shaft BMW) from the northern United States down the Pan-American Highway – similar to my own solo trip. They went as far south as they could travel on motorcycles – to Chepo – before turning back for the lack of any road. The information they gathered was that the only feasible way to get into South America from

Panama City was by ferry-boat, which was costly and had an erratic timetable.

They gave me their maps of Central and South America to illustrate their point while trying to convince me an overland route to South America was impossible. They told me the highway came to a sudden halt because of a relatively small but dense jungle area between Chepo and Colombia; shown on the map only as "proposed road".

For the first time I heard the words "Darien Jungle".

*   *   *   *   *

I now began to study the Inter-American maps every night, often for several hours at a sitting, to assure myself of the possibility or impossibility of driving through the jungle to South America.

My denial system was, to say the least, of gigantic proportions.

I began to envision a small dirt road, a beaten-down path, or even a slight trail that might go through the jungle and lead to somewhere in Colombia. I began convincing myself that if there were native Indians and animals living in the jungle, there *must* be some system of trails – no matter what the conditions might be. I felt confident I could force the dependable Honda through.

The more I thought about it, the more I was able to block out the advice of the bikers and convince myself that "it could be done". This fantasy soon became so real to me, my obsession so consuming, that sleep was nearly impossible.

Impatience made me want to confront this jungle, capturing the wilds of my imagination. I rushed the local mechanic through the necessary repairs to the Honda, said goodbye to my fellow American travelers, and started down the two hundred miles of dusty road toward the northern border of Panama to Panama City.

Almost as a preparation, this proved to be the most difficult two-hundred miles of my trip thus far. Huge rocks and boulders sometimes blocked the entire width of the unpaved road. Cows and other farm animals roamed the roads. Finely granulated dust, often three and four inches deep, kept my mouth gritty. And the water – in the form of streams – would cross the road in front of me without warning, giving my clothing a mummy-like look.

The road was every bit as difficult as my three American friends promised. It was the first real challenge I had faced thus far. If I could not pass this test, there was no hope of getting through the Darien Jungle. The difficult driving and the pulsating thoughts of the jungle adventure kept my mind in a frenzy, causing me to drive harder, longer, and more skillfully. Finally, I crossed the northern border into Panama and I was once again on paved highway.

I now felt a sense of accomplishment as I passed each village and land-mark, drawing me closer to Panama City and the Darien Jungle. The rising tide of obsession grew with each mile of Panamanian soil that passed under the knobbed tires of my motorcycle. To pass Panama City and just see the Darien Jungle now became the most important goal in my life. I wished time and space could be somehow transcended to start the test of my skills and knowledge against the dark jungle that lassoed my imagination and placed a noose around my thoughts.

The monotonous hours of driving had mesmerized my vision until I felt stationary while the scenery rushed past. Actually, I was beginning to hallucinate. I saw my upper body, arms, and hands somehow facing toward me, and it became impossible to know where my real hands and my imagined hands began or ended. My eyes had been fixed at a point only a few feet in front of my tires for so long that everything appeared in reverse. All the while my mind raced with the thoughts of excitement and adventure I imagined would come once inside the jungle. But a part of me knew when the road came to an end I would have to put my thoughts and fantasies into deeds and action.

Chapter 2

The road leading into Panama City began in the ultra-modern style of a four lane suspension bridge, spanning the entrance of the world famous canal. The Honda slowly carried me higher and higher over the narrow waterway that connects the two mighty oceans. I was much impressed by the height and length of the bridge and inspired by the tremendous view of the Pacific Ocean; giving my eyes the opportunity to un-focus.

Panama City was before me.

I was suddenly very happy to be living in the Twentieth Century and felt very self-satisfied for having just driven a motorcycle a distance of three thousand miles on the Pan American Highway. The excitement of the present was enough! For me, there was only the almighty NOW! I was living for the moment.

*　　*　　*　　*　　*

Driving into Panama City, I quickly became confused in an effort to find a place to sleep – not knowing whether to turn left into the American sector of the city, or turn right into the largely Panamanian portion. My habit of always living with the local people caused me to lean the Honda to the right and drive into the sweltering city where the tempo of the people was marked by a rocking rhythm characteristic of Afro-Latin culture. There were no outward signs or negative feeling from the resent riots over the control of the canal.

It was from this quarter I secured a cheap hotel and from where prostitution also flourished.

I roamed over Panama City searching for information helpful to my anticipated bid to get through the Darien Jungle and into South America. After two days of office-hopping through a bureaucratic maze of indifferent government officials, I knew no more about the Darien Jungle than its name.

The Information Bureau of the Panamanian Government offered nothing. I went to the American Military bases but was not allowed to enter. Officials at the American Canal Zone snubbed me.

In a desperate move, I marched into the office of the Darien Sub-Committee, organized by the Pan American Highway Congress to survey the "proposed" road through the jungle, and told them of my ambitions. They too looked at me as if I were crazy, shook my hand politely, told me it was impossible and to go back to the United States. They gave me no information.

I couldn't believe so many people living in a country as small as Panama could know so little about their land. Everyone spoke of the Darien as if it didn't exist, or as if it were in another country or another world. Yet it was only thirty-five miles from Panama City, their own capital, and made up nearly one-third of their entire country's land mass.

The one thing that everyone <u>did</u> know something about and agreed upon was the weather. They told me I was very lucky to be in Panama during their dry season when little or no rain fell.

Who believes in luck, anyway? Only children, fools, and alcoholics.

To attempt a trip into the jungle during any other time of the year, they said, would be virtually impossible because the summer months offered many inches of daily rainfall - over one hundred inches per season. I had about a month and a half.

This tiny shred of information served to increase my desire to travel through the Darien.

Finally, and to satisfy my natural tendency for disbelief, I left my equipment at the hotel and drove the Honda from Panama City on the last thirty-five miles of the Pan American Highway to Chepo for a firsthand look at the jungle.

The paved highway did in actual fact end in Chepo, as everyone had warned me and as the maps had shown. However, much to my delight, I discovered the Pan American Highway didn't stop there.

Further feeding my denial.

It continued southeastward in typical dirt-road fashion without the hint of an impending jungle.

Slowly and deliberately I drove through Chepo. The road was extremely dusty and spotted with hazardous rocks. And, I was forced to drive the dependable Honda through real water: through four knee deep rivers and six bubbling streams. Thereafter, the road worsened and the dust-covered vegetation began to shrink the width of the road.

I had driven a total of twenty-four miles past Chepo and my spirits were rising. But the terrain had gradually changed from farm-land to brush land, and finally to timberland that was slowly being cleared for homesteading.

Unknown to me at the time, I was observing the devastating consequences of the "slash and burn" method of clearing the land for agriculture. First, the larger trees are cut down by lumber companies, and then the remaining vegetation is cut down "slashed and burned" then cleared for farming. The usual crop is sugar cane. And, we now know, the soil eventually becomes barren and can no longer sustain plant life.

I was standing by the roadside of the village of El Llano enjoying the smiles of the local men with missing front teeth from sucking on sugar cane. The pungent smell of smoke from burning piles of fresh wood filled the air. Looking to the south I could see a wide river with rolling hills and the high closely cropped green trees of the jungle beyond. I stood there motionless for a full thirty minutes staring, wondering, and anticipating.

It was the Darien Jungle at last!

I wanted to raise my fist and yell: *"I'm gonna be with you soon!"* But I didn't.

I had seen enough for one day to heighten my optimism and to convince myself that sometimes most people <u>could</u> be wrong.

More fuel for the denial system.

After all, hadn't I already driven an almost effortless twenty four miles <u>past</u> Chepo? And the jungle, from what I could see of it, wasn't so ferocious and didn't impress me very much.

Driving the faithful Honda back to Chepo and then to Panama City, filled me with an airy smugness of knowing that I knew something that most other travelers didn't know, and that I had driven a motorcycle further south than anyone I knew or even heard about.

*   *   *   *   *

My confidence zooming, I scurried about the city seeking permission to enter and travel in the jungle region, Finally, after much haranguing and posturing, I was granted permission to enter the Darien Jungle – although with much reluctance by the

Panamanian Government. I also easily received a visa to enter the country of Colombia.

On the advice of the Panamanian Military and the police, I didn't purchase any firearms for protection. The Indians, they said, were often hostile toward outsiders.

As it turned out, the native Indians of Panama seemed more hostile toward Panamanians than white people; Norteamericanos.

Instead, I bought one box of twenty-two caliber shells and a few fish-hooks for bartering with the Cuna Indians.

I ran into a huge stumbling block, however, when I tried to obtain a *map* of the Darien Jungle. I went from office to office, and from official to official to no avail. There simply were no maps, detailed or otherwise, available for anyone.

Finally, and under a cloak of secrecy and connivance, I snuck my way onto one of the American Military bases on the outskirts of Panama City, and was able to talk my way into obtaining a (1:500,000) map of Panama covering the area roughly from Chepo to the northern border of Colombia. The Darien had never been surveyed, on the ground or from the air, so it wasn't a very detailed map, but it was the best to be had under the circumstances.

While on the American Military base, I "accidentally" ran into a Staff Sergeant from the 187th Unit of the 82nd Airborne Division. We chatted and agreed we had served together on Okinawa in the 503rd of the 82nd sometime during 1960 or 1961.

He was currently a Supply Sergeant and, much to my delight, gave me all the much-needed jungle equipment for jungle survival. Included were: jungle boots, hammock with mosquito net, machete, Halazone water purification tablets, a bayonet, some rope, and several boxes of C-Rations.

With a wry smile, he said what he couldn't give me was some common sense.

Interestingly, and just after that comment, he tried to dissuade me from going into the jungle, not because of the dangers, but because he had another agenda. He claimed to have aerial photos and the manifest of a downed U.S. military plane that crashed in the Andes Mountains in Colombia during WWII. He further claimed it contained a lot of gold bars, and wanted me and two or three other qualified parachutists to jump from a small plane onto the mountain near the crash site. Undetected, we could carry the gold in backpacks out of Colombia and into Panama where it could be sold on the black market for lots of American dollars.

Needless to say, it tickled the adventurousness – and greed – in me and was the strongest argument yet heard to keep me from the goal of traveling overland into South America.

I said no, and fortunately he didn't use the jungle equipment as ransom for an agreement to force me to go along with his scheme.

The next day I went to the American Embassy and told them of my intention to cross the Darien Jungle. They expressed extreme doubt but saw the impossibility of trying to change my mind. They did, however, introduce me to Thomas Willey, an American missionary working on the fringe area of the jungle.

Mr. Willey offered me the first real glimmer of hope by relating to me his personal knowledge of a small trail leading from the edge of the jungle to the Rio Bayano – about 35 miles from Chepo and thought there might be missionaries living there. He also knew of a guide who could lead me to the *next* river (the Chucunaque). From there, he surmised, it may be possible to meet Indians willing to lead me from village to village for most of the distance through the Darien into Colombia.

Everything seemed to be falling into place.

My plan was simple: I would box all excess personal belongings at the hotel where I was staying and ask them to forward it by mail to the American Embassy in Bogotá, Colombia.

I was really in fantasy-land to believe this sleazy hotel, with its' "women of the night" running around on every floor of the place, would actually follow through with forwarding my boxed belongings anywhere – let alone to another country.

I would then drive to Chepo and fill the Honda's gas tank to capacity, along with an extra one-gallon plastic container. That would be enough fuel to get the Honda to El Real – the capitol of the Darien about two hundred miles away – where Mr. Willey knew additional gasoline could be obtained. From El Real, I would, as Mr. Willey suggested, seek Cuna Indian guides to go from village to village until I got through to Colombia.

I had plenty of food in the boxes of military C-rations, and drinking water would not be a problem because of the many Halazone water purification tablets I carried. For shelter I carried a hammock with an enclosing mosquito net; and plenty of extra rope for climbing and pulling where necessary. With a full tank of gas and an extra 1-gallon plastic container strapped to the luggage-rack, I calculated this would be enough gas to get the Honda through the first 200 miles; hopefully to the village of El Real. I knew the Indians and the Panamanians used motor-powered canoes in the jungle, so gasoline would most likely be available.

Ha, ha. Again, the naivety syndrome.

Everything was ready. I merely had to wait for Mr. Willey to say when he would leave.

Fortunately, I didn't have to wait long. He was ready to return to his mission two days after our initial meeting, but would first show me to where the jungle actually began and introduce me to a guide, as he had promised. These two days were just enough time to organize my thoughts and prepare the equipment; i.e. have the Honda tuned, break-in the jungle boots, have the machete sharpened, and buy a few extra goodies. But after the sun went down the hours seemed to drag on and on, and I had difficulty sleeping.

Of course, listening to hallway bartering and the distinct sounds of paid–for-intimacy in nearby rooms didn't help. These long hours of nothingness were punctuated with excited thoughts of the adventure I was about to embark upon; and I desperately wanted someone with whom to share my excitement. These mood swings kept me awake until the rays of the morning sun filtered through the smoky air of the hot muggy room and the rhythmic sounds of the awakening city outside permitted sleep.

*   *   *   *   *

Finally, the time of departure arrived. I left Panama City for the last time on February 14th, 1965, riding the Honda and following Mr. Willey in his jeep.

The dusty ride to Chepo was uneventful – though the Honda followed behind the jeep as if it was being towed with a rope. Once in Chepo, as planned, I filled the Honda's gas tank to capacity.

Through Chepo and onward we continued down the rough dirt road past La Margarita and into El Llano; again crossing the four bridgeless rivers and the six rocky streams. But Mr. Willey and the jeep didn't stop at El Llano as I had previously done. He continued across another river and through the trees down a meandering dusty road for eight or nine miles with me in hot pursuit. After El Llano, the terrain was rolling hills studded with hundreds of hacked off tree stumps and patches of nearby brown grass covered with gritty dust blown off the road by passing vehicles.

At last we came to a stop beside a conglomerate of crude bamboo houses with thatched roofs of palm leaves. Mr. Willey stated this was Jenene – the last frontier!

My eyes searched the horizon in the bright, hot day through billowing waves of heat from the rays of the sun reflecting upward. Less than a mile from where I stood was an unending mass of green trees – the Darien Jungle. My stomach muscles contracted sharply. I jerked up, stretching my neck, trying to get a better view of it. But Mr. Willey distracted my attention by introducing me to the man who would be leading me to the Rio Bayano, on the first "leg" of my journey through the jungle. The guide, "Manuel", readily agreed to financial terms negotiated by Mr. Willey. He had shifty eyes and a crooked smile and I didn't feel completely comfortable with him, but he was all I had. He said we would leave the following morning before the sun rose while the new moon was still bright. We shook hands and Mr. Willey left Jenene, returning to Panama City. His parting words were: "If you are lucky you will run into a missionary couple on the Bayano."

My first effort at sleeping in a hammock was fruitless. I was now at the last frontier with the jungle in view. The once burning desire to get into the jungle turned into a somber reality as I stared into the great night sky and fought my insecurities. The hammock swung gently back and forth while the bright moon shone through the open door of my hut. But my thoughts always gravitated to that green void – the Darien Jungle – lying in wait for me, a short distance away. I was again biding my time, waiting for tomorrow as the moon moved inexorably across the silky-blue, moon-lit sky. My shakedown cruise was about to be severely tested.

*   *   *   *   *

But there was no tomorrow. A hastily prepared breakfast by candlelight, a nervous packing of equipment, and a moment of silence pushed Manuel and me down the narrowing road toward the spot - that fail-safe point where the dirt road ended and the jungle path began.

I would speed the Honda ahead several hundred yards through the finely granulated dust, and then stop to wait for my walking guide. Manuel wore a large round hat, lightweight cotton shirt and pants, and leather sandals. He carried only a machete in a sheath slung over his shoulder, a small bottle of water, and a shiny tin can of rice and meat in a cloth bag over the other shoulder. His steady walking pace would not be deterred by the alternating speed of the Honda.

Without warning the road that appeared before my headlight changed from soft dust to firm, freshly overturned earth that had obviously been widened by a bulldozer. It made the road easy to follow, but didn't last more than a thousand yards.

The grey dawn was beginning to get brighter and the encroaching trees were appearing closer and closer when the newly dug road came to an abrupt end on the near bank of a tiny stream just as the sun lifted itself into view.

Before me stood three hundred miles of raw, untamed jungle that towered above me and dwarfed my body as if I were in the swell of a great, green tidal wave. I suddenly felt the awful pangs of fear reminiscent of my fatherless childhood. It was a frozen fright of the unknown and caused me to feel unsure of myself for the first time since leaving the comfort of my California lifestyle. Was I man enough? Did I have what it would take to do this? And yet there was the competing feeling of adventurousness racing through my body and electrifying my mind, trying to overcome my fears, doubts, and insecurities to help me take that first step, that leap into the unknown. I always used this sense of adventurousness to drive out the fear and commit to a goal. And, even though I now felt enslaved by *this* commitment, I didn't want to turn back.

Manuel just stood there before the tall green jungle with his arms akimbo and his head turned toward me. He spoke not a word, but his eyes produced the defiant stare of a frontiersman as if to say, "Are you going in or not? Or are you just another soft *gringo* from the north?" My own glance ricocheted off his consistent stare and focused on the jungle directly in front of me. The trees were growing so close together they seemed impenetrable, and the green color of the trees, leaves, shrubbery, and grass so lush, that it appeared fused into one curtain of vegetation with only a few dead branches and yellow flowers clashing with the overall verdure. I could see into the thicket no further than twenty or thirty yards down the path.

A soft breeze carried a curious smell into my nostrils. The sound of a mimicking bird reached my ears and echoed through the trees in a shrill, but inviting tone. My right hand reached out to fondle a large moist leaf. The exotic jungle atmosphere filled my mind with exciting thoughts, and I knew I would have to enter. The need for action and involvement overcame any and all fears and indecision.

With confidence still in doubt, uncertain of my chances in the forbidden terrain, I filled my lungs to capacity, jumped back on the motorcycle and nodded to Manuel to lead the way. With a sudden burst of crackling mufflers, I accelerated the motorcycle's engine and followed the Panamanian up a sharp creek embankment, through an opening in the trees and into the maze of undergrowth that was the beginning of the Darien Jungle.

*   *   *   *   *

The narrow path was hard, uneven, dark earth that quickly jolted me back to reality.

Down the trail I went, following my guide, bobbing up and down on the motorcycle's cushioned seat, trying desperately to hold onto the handlebars. Immediately, I found the width of the handlebars made my knuckles vulnerable to the protruding branches of the trees and prickly bushes. Soon bleeding flesh showed through my torn leather gloves from the constant pulling and scraping of the vegetation sticking out like sharp sticks in a gauntlet. I grabbed the light jacket from my saddle-bags and pulled it on to protect my exposed arms and neck.

At regular intervals the Honda and I would "spill", and I would find myself lying in the bushes beside the motorcycle, its hot engine gasping for life. Several hours had gone by when I realized it was becoming more and more difficult to shift from neutral to first gear and second gear. I had gone less than a mile when the Honda refused to move forward under its own power. I could not shift gears.

Manuel hovered around as I knelt over the Honda, vainly trying to get it in gear, any gear. His body language showed visible impatience, and I knew he had doubted the success of my journey from the beginning. As the father of several small children and a farmer, I was certain he was anxious to return; and was just being my guide because he needed the cash.

Using an old piece of brown paper bag and my pencil, he drew a crude map of the immediate area and illustrated how to follow this trail to the Rio Silugandi – then on to the Rio Bayano. I shall never forget the wry smile on Manuel's face as he gave me a cocky salute goodbye and began walking back toward Jenene.

Alone again!

I just sat there for a while on a mound of hard dark soil, alone and not knowing what to do. Straightening my back I raised my head to survey the surrounding area, shielded from the brilliant Panamanian sun by the layers of foliage. For the first time I had an opportunity to experience the jungle from the inside out – rather than the outside in. The depth of the green textured leaves and plants mixed with the many shapes of the brown trunks and branches fed my eyes with beauty unknown to me before. Unusual flower fragrances stimulated my nostrils while the pungent odor of the terra firma mixed with decaying layers of fallen plant life became sharpened without the interference of the only external influence - the Honda's exhaust fumes.

It was like a new world: the emerald-green leaves seemed to blink at the early sunlight reflecting off the microscopic particles in the air as the canopy of green moved unevenly in the early morning breeze. Tiny dribbles of water still clung to the lower leaves glistening like pearls. The soft rustling of leaves, the humming of the insects, and the occasional mocking calls of a bird were new and exotic sensations, amplified by my aloneness.

The dead and dying were there too. Rotten trees trunks, mangled branches, and dried vegetation being pulled by gravity into the dark rich soil; pregnant with new life.

Without changing position I stretched out my arm and snapped off the stem of a reddish-orange flower and lowered my face into it for a closer look and a greater smell.

I was now secretly happy my guide had deserted me, for I selfishly wanted to enjoy the rapture of the jungle alone; and prove to myself that I could do it alone. For a while I felt as if I wanted to stay in that same spot forever. But each time I made a sweeping glance of the staggering landscape surrounding me, my eyes always returned to the alien Honda parked on the hardened trail beside me.

As my thoughts returned to the situation at hand, the relaxing time was spent enjoying the natural surroundings seeming to ease my stress and allowing me to think more clearly. My non-mechanical mind eventually understood that the clutch-cable, already six months old, had been badly stretched. The constant braking, changing gears, and the accelerating to traverse the irregular terrain were enough to strain the most even-tempered cable.

I rummaged through the saddle-bags searching for the spare cable, and spent more than an hour replacing the old with the new. The grease and oil from the old cable did no good to my already bruised and scratched hands, but the clutch was again operating, and I cautiously continued down the path alone; still bobbing up and down on the cushioned seat.

Several hundred yards after the clutch cable was replaced, I was confronted with my first major obstacle in the jungle: a near emptied creek-bed with deep, soft banks of black mud fifteen feet wide. I found it almost impossible to stand unaided in the soft mud without slowly sinking in. Obviously, the narrow tires and the hundred and fifty pound weight of the Honda would easily slice into the mud and sink the vehicle beyond my reach – or my power to extract it. A quick up and down search of the immediate creek area for an easier spot to cross the yielding soft earth proved futile.

There was no other way around it! I had to somehow cross this crack in the earth where it intersected with the trail.

The sun was high overhead and the air was thick, so I stripped to the waist and began my preparations for the crossing. I started chopping down all the nearby broad-back palms, thick grass, and any type of vegetation lending broad support for the wheels of the Honda. The free-swinging of the machete gave me a feeling of exuberant energy as it whisked through air neatly severing the firm, moist plants. The large, round flat leaves seemed to hover for an instant after being separated from the mother stalks then falling defiantly to the ground.

I became so involved with the stroking power of the machete that for a while the immediate problems of crossing the soft banks of the creek bed were out of my mind. However, stepping over the mounds of green debris brought me back to the task at hand. I began dragging the fallen plants to the creek-bed and laying them in crisscross fashion several layers deep. Soon a green carpet of palm leaves, grass, and thick brush stretched before me from the top of the near bank, across the bottom, and to the top of the bank on the opposite side.

Starting the engine, I began slowly walking the motorcycle, in neutral, down the layers of leaves with the aid of the hand brake to control the speed – all the while trying to maintain my own sense of balance on the slippery vegetation.

The method succeeded until the Honda reached the bottom of the gulley and I started up the other side.

The back tire began to slip and spin. I quickly released the clutch and squeezed on the gas attempting to keep the vehicle moving up the embankment. But to no avail! The back wheel fish-tailed and only spun faster as the knobbed tires chewed away at the soft flesh of the green plants. Gradually, a black, oily looking solution of mud and water seeped its way between the leaves and stalks, slowly enclosing the sinking rear wheel.

I tried pushing the bike, then pulling on some nearby branches with my left hand while my right hand accelerated the gas handle. But the Honda remained stationary as if held by an invisible tether.

In a vain attempt I tried speed. But the rear wheel began spinning so fast smoke poured up to my nostrils with the unmistakable smell of burning rubber. The rear wheel of the motorcycle was now firmly entrenched in two feet of mud and ground leaves and could remain standing upright without assistance. I tried various combinations of starting and stopping the turning of the wheel, rocking back and forth, pushing and pulling. Nothing seemed to work!

Then in one supreme effort, I hoisted the back of the motorcycle out of the sticky black goop by the luggage rack and onto fresh palms. In the process, I found *myself* stuck thigh-deep in the black mud. As I tried to raise my legs, the weight of my body caused me to be sucked in deeper.

What a sight it must have been: there I was, firmly anchored up to my thighs in sucking mud while my arms were raised high trying to support and balance a motorcycle, with no other person within miles.

Humor aside, the air was mucky and hot, causing large balls of sweat to pour down my forehead, burning my eyes. It was mid-day yet I found myself in near darkness from the canopy of the lavishly ornamented branches covering the ditch. There was an omnipresent contradiction between the brilliance of the greenery and the deepness of the black mud – beautiful to look at but discouraging to be in.

For a moment I was panicky.

A strong urge to climb out of that black hole, forget about the whole scheme of going to South America, and run back to civilization overcame me.

What am I doing here, anyway? Nobody in their right mind would be here with me – let alone do it solo.

But this was my first real test. This was the first trial to prove if I were strong and tenacious enough to make it. I refused to give up so soon without a real struggle on my shakedown cruise.

The maneuver of freeing my legs from the muck while holding onto the motorcycle proved interesting. I allowed the Honda to fall gently over on the bed of leaves and stems while forcing the weight of my upper body partially over the motorcycle and partially on fresh leaves until I was freed. The same process of lifting the rear wheel onto a fresh bed of leaves while freeing myself from the slime continued for nearly an hour until I eventually got the machine on firm earth once again.

One more slippery trip back across the broken bed of foliage (without the motorcycle, of course) to retrieve the unloaded gear was necessary before I continued down the trail.

But rather than load the extra gear back on the Honda, I carried it a hundred yards or so down the trail, at the same time clearing the path of obstructions marring the approach of the motorcycle. I walked the Honda to the spot where the gear was lying on the trail, and began a routine of walking the Honda and carrying the equipment ahead, that was to continue throughout the time that I kept the motorcycle.

This slow means of progress went on until I noticed the shrinking distance between the barely visible sun and the horizon. As I approached the knoll of a small hill, my first day in the Darien Jungle was nearing its end.

Somehow the setting sun appeared massive and flaming with its reddish-orange glow saluting the day and all that was done. The evening glowed with the intensity of liquid steel, pouring its richness over the countryside, filling the jungle with the penetrating radiance of a Dali landscape. I was forced again and again to stop and catch the view as I prepared my first campsite. I didn't want it to disappear; but inch by inch it faded from view.

*   *   *   *   *

As the dusk settled around me, the jungle became eerily quiet. Once more I became aware of my aloneness. There was no place to go, nobody to talk with, and nobody to hear about my struggles of the day.

Someone will come down this trail any minute now – someone, I know. I am just sure they will.

But there was only an empty blackness as the night arrived – a reflection of the darkness inside.

Physically exhausted, I lay in the strung hammock with my hands folded on my chest, relaxing my muscles. My ears now became supersensitive to the movements in the jungle. I began to hear strange sounds never heard before. There was a distant groan or a nearby crack of tree rubbing together. Each time I would jerk my head up from the hammock to survey the darkness surrounding me, convinced that sooner or later another human being would come down the trail and say: "Hi."

I was afraid to go to sleep. With the inevitable darkness came the only audience I was to have – the concert of screaming insects of the jungle night. Crickets, countless whippoorwills, and the buzzing mosquitoes sounded their appreciation of the damp black night. But they kept me awake. The muscles of my body were much too sore and tired to permit sleep. To add to the insomnia an early luminous moon appeared through the staccato of jungle trees; and stayed for most of the night.

During the first night in the jungle, I was to sleep no more than an hour.

*   *   *   *   *

On my second day in the Darien Jungle, before the sun came fully into view, I continued down the trail toward the Rio Silugandi. As on the previous day I carried my equipment forward for several hundred yards and clearing the path of branches, rocks and fallen trees. It was shortly after sunrise, while standing at the base of a long sloping hill that I encountered my second major obstacle. There was a fifteen foot gap in the trail which, at first, appeared as if it had been opened by an earthquake.

This eroded break in the trail was a cleft twice as deep as it was wide, and had probably been caused by a once-raging stream of water from a torrential rain; but was now dry. I footed my way to the bottom of the opening and could easily see the steepness would be precarious even for a mule, and impossible for a motorcycle.

A bridge was the only answer. I had to build a bridge, and decided to start immediately.

Having never been in the Boy Scouts and with no engineering education, I had to rely on instinct and the memories of old Tarzan movies for the construction. I climbed down and up the embankments to the other side of the gap and quickly decided to use two parallel logs, approximately 10 inches in diameter, as the mainstays for the span. I chose a tall firm tree with few lower branches situated close to the opening in the trail and long enough to reach the opposite side when felled.

With the fierce determination of a lumber-jack, I began hacking away at the soft moist timber with the machete, after having first chopped a notch at about a 45 degree angle on the opposite side of the tree in the direction I wanted it to fall.

I'm remembering the days when I worked as a choker-setter in a lumber camp in Oregon in 1963.

Flat chips of sticky yellow wood easily flaked about me radiating an aroma of spring flowers, and forming a pile of shavings several inches deep around my boots. As the tree weakened, I pushed it toward the other side; hoping for a right angle position to the gap.

The nearly rootless tree fought its way down through the ill-groomed branches and surrounding vines. It struck the ground with a thunderous boom, at a neat right angle to the dry creek bed.

Returning to the motorcycle side, I chose a tree of similar size and distance from the gap and repeated the cutting process – but without the same results. This time, instead of the deep resonant sound of a tree hitting the ground, the shrilling noise of splintering wood pierced the soft air. The tree had broken off near the center of the gorge. Luckily the bottom half of the broken tree was just long enough to reach across the gap. Tying a rope to the splintered end of the log I managed to pull and drag it onto the bank and align it about 30 inches beside the first log.

With the two main supports now in place, I chopped off all the unnecessary branches to clear the approach route leading to the bridge of broken tree limbs and other debris.

Next was the arduous task of laying the surface of the bridge. Cutting and gathering fresh branches two to three inches in diameter and tying them to the logs using small flexible vines. Using rocks and mud, I built an on-ramp and an off-ramp to the makeshift bridge to make it easily accessible to the wheels of the Honda. I cut and drove wooden pegs into the ground at the 4 corners of the supports to prevent sideway slippage.

It took eight hours.

I walked back and forth over the completed bridge, my bridge, and multiple times with the air of an elated engineer checked for weak branches, loose vine tie-downs or sharp branches that might puncture a tire.

Satisfied the bridge would accept the weight of the Honda and me; I stripped the motorcycle of everything unnecessary and started the engine. But rather than attempt to *ride* the Honda to the other side, I decided to walk it across the bridge to be certain the weight of me and the motorcycle was close to one of the main logs hoping for a good "weight displacement". Getting the Honda up the ramp and onto the bridge was tricky. With a sudden burst of power the Honda and I were on the bridge, then quickly near the midway point across.

The Honda refused to move forward over one of the larger uneven branches tied to the main stays. As if suspended in mid-air, I fought to maintain upright stability – the Honda could fall off the left side and I off the right side, or we could both fall off the same side. If the Honda fell into the gorge it would be a disaster and impossible for me alone to lug out. All my hopes would be dashed.

What to do? I was in the moment, fully focused; temples throbbing! It was the *here and now*.

It seemed to last forever. I held on tightly.

My reflexes took command.

Instinctively I let the clutch bar fly fully open while, at the same time, opening the gas throttle as far as it would turn. In a loud squeak, the front tire quickly bolted over the hump of tied branch and we scooted over the remaining eight feet of bridge before I could blink my eyes. Near the last two feet of bridge, the rear wheel slipped completely off the superstructure. But by that time I was already once again on solid ground and quickly motored to a level spot in the trail – heaving a huge sigh of relief.

*   *   *   *   *

Down the trail I went riding and walking the Honda, stopping occasionally for a rest or drink of water.

I found myself beginning to daydream a lot. The solitude was beginning to weigh heavily on my mind. I had not seen another person in 48 hours.

I've always enjoyed being alone, reveling in my thoughts and fantasies. But this! This is different. Before I could always walk outside that doorway of my mind and see people; someone, anyone. Now I had no choice. I had to be alone. All I have is backward memories and forward fantasies. I'm beginning to analyze each thought, every feeling, and all movement with microscopic closeness. Why am I thinking that? Which feeling is this? What caused me to do that?

I laughed aloud when I caught myself walking thirty or forty feet to the left or right of the main trail to urinate, or digging a hole to bury my feces; as if someone was watching to make certain it was done properly.

There were moments when I would stare at the pictures in my wallet, becoming happy to see a familiar face or sad to the point of tears because I could not share with them my experiences. I wanted to be with my mother, sister, and brother, and my "west coast" family – the Hinkle's. What would they say to me if any one of them were standing here beside me?

Slowly I began to realize I had been *inhibited* for most of my life and my every action was motivated by the world from which I had come. Consequently I began to practice thinking more spontaneous while allowing myself unfiltered feelings; especially to childhood secrets, now erupting to the surface by the oppressive loneliness.

One of the first things I did was scream and yell as long and as loud as I possibly could until I was exhausted. Once I even removed all my clothing and just walked around, jumped and ran through the surrounding jungle vegetation. The multitude of conspiring insects ensured that this behavior didn't last very long. Another time I rolled over and over in the dust and black dirt of the trail giving myself permission to get as dirty as possible.

This *feels* good! But it's probably not a good idea.

Primal Therapy?

But then once again I returned to the serious business of competing with the jungle terrain.

*   *   *   *   *

Always it was the afflictions and trying experiences that diverted my feelings of loneliness to thoughts and actions of survival.

On the third day, I stood gazing upward as the trail lead up a hill towering forty to fifty feet above me. I scrambled to the top to survey the route which I might be able to drive the Honda. Each step was slippery like grease. Returning to the bottom I decided to be bodacious and drive straight up the hill. Stripped of extra gear, the engine running wide open, glued to the seat, up we went.

The first burst of power carried us only half way up the hill. It was as if the Honda had come to the end of its rope, like a dog on a leash, and I was the dog and gravity was the leash. The 150 horsepower engine just didn't have enough power to take us further. The bike toppled over to the right, threw me further to the right. Desperately I held fast to the handlebars stuck straight into the air; hoping to prevent the machine from sliding back down the hill.

In that instant the motorcycle quickly gained movement and began sliding down the slippery stony slope on its side, pulling me down with it. After sliding on my stomach, knees and feet, I finally managed to stop the motorcycle only after it had nearly reached the bottom. Engine running and wheels revolving, the cycle lay there like a wounded animal unable to escape its predator.

Regaining my sense of balance and direction, I righted the motorcycle for a second attempt at the hill hoping the experience of the first ride would help. But the same disaster repeated. Finally, I decided on a more logical approach. If it was impossible to reach the top by the most direct route, perhaps an *indirect* course would succeed. I began digging a series of steps, or platforms, (six in all) in a zigzag pattern about ten feet apart to the top of the hill. I dug at the hardened earth with my machete, six inch knife, sticks, and rocks – anything that would penetrate the hardened soil. At each step I flattened a space just large enough for the motorcycle and myself to stop momentarily before progressing onto the next level upward. As an added precaution I tied a rope around the handlebars and a nearby tree at the next higher level to prevent any slippage.

Inching my way up, I drove the Honda to the first platform from a standing position alongside. At the third level, the bike fell onto my right leg, the manifold scorching my trousers and giving me a first degree burn on the inside of my knee.

At every level thereafter the Honda would tilt, fall, or get out of my control until I was ready to explode from the tiring frustration.

After much toil, sweat, and profanity, I reached the top with sustainable damage – one sheared-off mirror, a broken brake handle, a badly dented gas tank, five bleeding knuckles, torn pants, a burnt knee, and shattered nerves.

But, I had reached the top.

For the first time since entering the jungle I was exhausted and hungry. I haphazardly tore open the cardboard box tied to the back of the Honda and took out one of 12 boxes of daily C-rations. Using the P-38, I opened a can of eggs and ham and began eating.

Whoever invented this P-38 was brilliant! But this is totally crazy – and funny at the same time. Here I am eating a can of military C-Rations and enjoying it! It actually tastes good. I ate tons of this stuff on every march and every bivouac during my 3 year military career and absolutely hated it. Thought it was greasy tasteless crap. Now I like it. Change or die.

It was so good I opened another one – pork and beans this time. I must have really been hungry because it tasted delicious. The cocoa bar was dry and very un-chocolate-like but I knew it was nutritious so I ate it, and topped off the meal with grape jam on 2 stale crackers. A long drink of cool water from the canteen, and a short rest in the trunk of a banyan tree in the unusually fresh breeze and I was ready to go.

The food and rest restored my ebbing spirit and I continued down the lonely trail – sometimes riding the Honda, sometimes walking it.

Why is there nobody here? Surely, some people must walk this path. It looks so well used.

Scouting ahead of the motorcycle, I discovered that my path was blocked by a giant tree that had recently fallen. Knowing it would take days to hack through the three feet of wood and wide enough for the bike to get through; the choice to go around was evident.

Back bent, I painstakingly cleared a path out of the fallen branches and growing vegetation to the left of the blocked trail where the jungle growth was less dense. Chopping through thick limbs, moving decayed logs, broken branches, the semi-circular route to the other side of the trail was completed in about an hour. The tires of the Honda were pricked and cut several times by the stubs of the many bushes that stuck out of the ground like wooden nails. Fortunately, the inner tubes survived the pricking. I never thought of bringing a spare tire or tube.

Around the tree I continued down the trail, literally fighting the jungle for each few yards of forward progress. Every fifty to a hundred feet the front tire of the Honda encountered another fallen tree blocking its forward motion. The fallen trees, the endless procession of hills, sharp ridges, and deep gullies of the jungle landscape kept me in a constant state of acrobatics with the motorcycle. The deeper I penetrated into the Darien the more difficult and more numerous the obstacles became. I longed for a hundred feet of straight and level terrain to ride the Honda without interruptions, obstacles, or detours. As the trail became more and more difficult to follow, the jungle became more and more unruly. The clutch cable showed signs of being frayed and stretched.

As the green grew closer around me and as I became physically more strained, I tried to cheer myself up by comparing the Darien Jungle I was experiencing to my ideal of how I had thought the jungle might be. The visual beauty far exceeded my expectations, but to forging through its thickness, scrambling up and down the uneven terrain, and tolerating such humid weather I had not anticipated. The tasteless grit and dirt, the biting insects, and the scratches and bruises were all more than I bargained for.

The jungle is the epitome of nonconformity.

*   *   *   *   *

After days of swearing, sweating, scratching, and bleeding my way through the denseness for every yard forward, I finally reached the first major objective: the Rio Silugandi. At first I was stunned by the sight of the flat smooth surface of the shiny water against the irregular background of jungle roughness. I stood on a hill nearly fifty yards away, uncertain if what I was seeing was a mirage or not.

As I approached, I heard the murmuring sounds and focused on the glistening water easing over the slippery pebbles.

I ran down the long hill and jumped into the cool, clear water in triumphant glee. I splashed about, throwing the water into the air, onto my face, and down my shirt as I held my head back and looked at the slice of clean blue sky through the crack in the jungle canopy up and down the river.

This is really a <u>creek</u> by most standards. It's only about 50 feet wide. The Susquehanna River of my Pennsylvania childhood is a mile wide in some parts.

Never had water been so needed, or soap more cleansing. Naked, I scrubbed my body from head to toe, then again from toe to head. Once again were my body and mind clear. I could think. I could plan, and I could dream.

That evening, I sat beside the Silugandi on a log, grayed by the endurance of time, thinking again of South America. Still naked, as my body drank in the cool air, I felt at peace with myself and the jungle world around me. The sun wallowed in a few scattered clouds on what I could see of the horizon. A hopeful fishing line broke the surface of the quiet backwater as a weaving water-snake swam under the string. I crawled into the sleeping bag and laid the machete next to me; my only means of protection, and a constant reminder that this was not Utopia.

*   *   *   *   *

The morning saw me busily filling in the log-infested bank with rocks and mud in hopes of gaining a smooth passage for the Honda to enter and cross the shallow river. I tried to visualize the path the bike would follow as I waded through the thigh-deep water; clearing the proposed route of large rocks and jammed branches on the bottom. The steady force of the current and the depth of the water were the two primary concerns. Nonetheless, remembering the Honda already crossed many rivers and creeks, I felt confident these obstacles could be surmounted.

I stripped the bike of everything except the essentials and piled all my gear and the motorcycle extras at the water's edge.

Sitting on the bare Honda, I roared down the fifteen foot embankment, doggedly trying to maintain stability over the rocks, mud, and pieces of wood leading into the river. Headlong we went into the river, only to be sucked under the water like a broken ship. Quickly dismounting, I lost control of the nearly submerged machine. In a muffled huff, the engine stopped.

I pushed and pulled the motorcycle forward with all the strength the fibers of my muscles could muster. The wheels inched ahead a few rocks at a time. At one point the current became so over-powering it caused the Honda to tilt over and go completely under water, nearly dragging me with it. Temporarily letting go of the handlebars, I dove into the water and again righted the vehicle. Only the headlight and the handlebars were above water.

Close to the point of panic, I nervously shuffled around to the down-stream side of the bike, fighting my way through the steady current, hoping my body would lend support to the tilting machine. The rocks were so slippery against my soft rubber soled boots and the motorcycle tires for much of the distance across that we merely slid across the slimy bottom surface diagonally. The current's strength caused the front wheel to careen downstream far off the expected straight line course. Encountering several large rocks, it was necessary for me to trudge to the front wheel, lift it past each rock, then use the luggage rack to pull the rear wheel along, while at the same time trying to keep the motorcycle in an upright position.

The effort to cross the river seemed like a hopeless cause. The handlebars barely moved forward while the current pushed us further and further downstream. But the fear of losing the Honda to the river gave me strength until I guessed I was nearly at the half-way point in waist-deep water.

Painstakingly slow, I got closer and closer to the opposite side, and with the approaching bank my efforts multiplied as my will and determination again surpassed my skills. Every spark of energy was directed toward the goal of getting the Honda onto dry ground. So magnetized was my fierce effort that even after reaching the opposite bank, I continued pushing the motorcycle onward for several yards extra, despite the rough rocky bank.

Coughing and exhausted, I flung the bike against the nearest tree and sunk to the ground, gasping for air and partially blinded by the salty stream of sweat running down my forehead.

Somehow the crossing of the Silugandi River did not have the same exhilarating and conquering effect as had my past goals and accomplishments. A strange feeling and cloud of guilt hung over my consciousness as if I had done something wrong – as if I had done the Honda an injustice. The motorcycle had been completely submerged for at least fifteen or twenty minutes during the crossing, and had stopped running long before reaching midway across.

Did I kill it? Is the Honda dead? Is this to be another loss for me?

I jumped up and tried the electric starter, but it only hummed in agitated diminishing monotony. I gave the battery a thirty minute rest and tried again. Again and again I pressed the black plastic starter button until it refused even the slightest signal.

Moving with the swiftness of a surgeon on a dying patient, I quickly switched to the kick-starter and began pumping feverishly with my leg. I tried all the combinations of kick-starter, manipulating the choke, and again on the electric starter. Nothing worked! The harshness of the terrain made it virtually impossible for me to start the engine by pushing. So I rested.

Checking and rechecking the points, plugs, battery, fuel lines, everything an amateur like me could fathom. Each item appeared lightly dampened but serviceable. The electric-starter regained a bit of life but quickly petered out. Again I pumped and pumped the kick-starter until my thigh was burning and my ankle bruised by the constant flicking of the retracting starter pedal.

I somehow sensed it was the end for the motorcycle. It had survived the flat plains of Mexico, the mountains of Central America, the depths of creeks and rivers, and the jungle thus far. The clutch cable could barely produce tension.

Why now? Why did it have to stop running at such a crucial place?

Time was not so important, nor the weather, nor money. To be stranded literally in the middle of "no-man's land" without any possibility of recovery or assistance was devastating. There was nowhere to go, nobody to help, and nothing else I could do for the Honda.

All my hopes and dreams were vanished by the river-crossing. I knew it!

I was overcome with the frustration of a defeat that hung over my head like a black cloud. Suddenly I hated the motorcycle with a passion.

It was a stupid idea anyway. Who would believe it possible for a man to drag a motorcycle through the length of the Darien Jungle?

My rising anger grew until I even cursed myself for leaving the comforts of Southern California and subjecting myself to these hardships.

Damn Kerouac!

To satisfy the frustration, I kicked the defenseless motorcycle with my soggy boot and knocked it to the ground. It rocked back and forth for a moment, while the front wheel revolved slowly around like the second hand of a clock.

I stood there and shouted abuses as loud and as long as I could, mostly toward myself for failing. *That* part of the shakedown cruise didn't work!

Turning away in anguish I checked the map. With the motorcycle finished, the next best thing was to attempt to return it, and me, to civilization. With the motor conked out, I knew it would be a useless struggle trying to push it back out of the jungle. The Rio Bayano was three miles due east on the map - double that would be about six "jungle miles". And with the day still in the early hours, I could possibly walk there before sundown.

The map also showed an apparently small village, Boca Playita, where the Bayano River and the Playita River merged. Once there, perhaps I could get some help retrieving the motorcycle by canoe. Down the river was La Capitanna to where a short paved road leads directly to Chepo. But the Honda was no longer important. I just wanted to get out of here and return to civilization.

On an impulse I began calculating how far the motorcycle and I had traveled since entering the jungle. I had scrawled down the reading on the odometer as I entered the jungle with my guide. But having been previously occupied by the struggle with the motorcycle on the harsh terrain, the matter of mileage seemed unimportant until now

I wrote down the mileage figure above the one noted as I entered the jungle. I couldn't believe my eyes. I double checked and triple checked the figures. They were correct. I had traveled exactly *four and four-tenth miles* in those four long days!

Chapter 3

Instead of starting the walk to the Rio Bayano, I experienced a fitful sleep that night beside the now-wasted motorcycle. My mind was warped with indecision. Each thought was flooded with a hundred images and ideas, each with endless scenarios.

What's next? Where do I go from here?

More vain attempts to get the motorcycle started fully convinced me the motorcycle was no longer an option. I had made no substitute plans, no alternate course of action that didn't include the bike. My only ambition had been to travel to Colombia and into all of South America. Never once did I give any thought to the possibility the motorcycle would not, or could not, make the entire journey.

My future loomed before me like the labyrinth that was the dark Darien Jungle around me.

*   *   *   *   *

Sometime during the restless night I arrived at the decision to abide by my earlier decision to return to civilization and, if possible, get the Honda to Panama City to have it repaired. I squinted at the map in the early morning light trying to understand the pencil lines drawn by my shifty-eyed guide showing the directions to the Rio Bayano. The only hope for retrieving the Honda, of course, rested on the possibility of getting a canoe or some type of river boat to come up the Rio Silugandi from the Rio Bayano, then to head downstream to the small village of La Capitana.

But my interest in the Honda was waning.

I absolutely hate anything mechanical that does not work!

For the moment, however, I just wanted to feel some contact with other humans – back to the real world where real people were doing real things.

But I had to first assess all my food, supplies, and equipment, decide what to take and what to leave behind, and how to carry everything.

I emptied the luggage rack, saddle bags, the smaller bags from within, and took everything from my pockets to lie on the spread poncho. Including the boxes of C-rations, there was a two foot mound of stuff spread over the flattened poncho.

WOW! I had no idea I had <u>this</u> much junk with me.

I couldn't possibly carry <u>everything </u>without weighing myself down to near immobility – and raising the risk of not making it at all.

Also, an opportunity might never again present itself for a return trip up the Silugandi for the Honda, hence losing anything left behind to corrosion or others walking the trail. But at this point only thoughts of survival dominated my mind; only the bare necessities could be carried. But…if there was the slightest chance an item would be needed I knew it must be taken, regardless of the physical hardship to be endured.

Disregarding personal comfort, I took decisive action and assembled my survival kit. Ruthlessly the pile of food and gear was reduced to the bare essentials – as best as I could discern. Next was the problem of how to carry everything. I unhooked the saddlebags and buckled the straps together, forming a convenient slot between the bags for my head to slip through; one bag rested solidly on my back, the other on my chest. For sleeping, I rolled the hammock, mosquito-net, and light-weight blanket into the poncho – cowboy style – and wrapped a ten foot piece of rope around it with a long loop for easy carrying over my shoulder. I had the G.I. canteen for water on a pistol-belt around my waist, and plenty of Halazone tablets.

I grabbed the empty saddle-bags and stuffed them with as many cans of C-rations as possible, leaving only enough space for the first-aid kit, a snake-bite kit, my passport and what little money I had left.

God, I only have six $25 Travelers Checks, $12.00 in American dollars, and a few <u>centesimos</u> in change left to my name. Oh well, I don't have to worry about <u>that</u> until I get out of here.

An extra pair of socks topped off each bag. Before strapping them closed, I stuffed the small box of twenty-two rifle shells and fish hooks into one side, purchased in Panama City, at the behest of several people, for barter with the Indians I might encounter. I now felt ready to continue; confident I could survive several weeks in the jungle – if necessary.

Tossing the compacted leather bags over my head, I tested the strength of the straps and weight of the load. I slung the rope loop of tied sleeping gear over my head onto my right shoulder, as the roll rested at my left side. It wasn't comfortable by any stretch, but could be endured. I gently rested the Panamanian straw hat on my head of greasy-hair and picked up the last and most important item of equipment – the stout machete.

One thing I've learned very quickly so far: survival in the jungle <u>without</u> a machete, and a file to sharpen it, is impossible.

Shaking my body several times to settle the heavy load, I took several deep breaths and was off. Compass in the left hand, machete in my right, and the map in my back pocket, I started down the trail for the Bayano on a south-easterly course.

*   *   *   *   *

I walked only a few steps when the Honda, lying next to the steady flow of the Silugandi River, acted like a magnet trying to draw me back. I wanted to leave without looking – but couldn't. For several minutes my eyes remained focused on the lifeless black and chrome machine – a machine that had carried me for many months through cities, mountains, hills, prairie, plains, and jungle – thousands of miles. I felt a certain grief and sadness that comes with the loss of a love, something intangible.

<u>After many trans-ocean sailboat trips, I once thought I loved the sea. However, I came to realize and believe what Yukio Mishima said in his novel "The Sailor Who Fell From Grace With the Sea". The sea, he said, will never love you in return.</u>

I blinked my red eyes several times and went off into the jungle, once again filled with energy and the excitement of adventure.

At first I welcomed the pricks of the pointy thorns, the stinging whip of the slapping branches and the taste of the gritty jungle dirt – as if in self-punishment for my defeat of failing to drive the Honda to Colombia and South America. But the surrounding natural beauty of the living, breathing plants quickly overcame the feeling of defeat.

The weather-hardened trail was easy to follow at first, and traveling on foot without the responsibilities of a motorcycle, made it easy to move forward. It soon became a game to dodge the protruding branches, as I lightheartedly ambled down the trail, completely enchanted by the vividness of the natural green. There are *so* many shades of green; and an infinite number of shapes and textures, but no people.

I was thoroughly enjoying my new-found freedom.

More and more I came to realize the lightness of being without the Honda.

Now, with only the responsibility of me, my once drained confidence had returned, as I buoyantly stepped down the grassy trail; even taking extra swipes with the machete at plants blocking the way forward. It was as if a very large log had been lifted off my back. Now I was just me against the jungle – and I was ready. Every step forward was easy, and one I knew I would not have to retrace. There would be no more pulling, straining, scratching, fighting, for every foot forward of terra firma.

Or so I thought at the time.

Habit forced me to visualize how the motorcycle would fare if it were still on the trail with me. At first it would have been very comfortable; at least more so than the last mile or two.

The trail was grassy and smooth, with only a few minor obstructions and gullies to slow my movement. But gradually and almost without notice, the greenness of the jungle began to squeeze in slowly, like the jaws of a giant flesh-eating Venus flytrap in slow motion. Thin strands of vines hung from above as sticky plants popped up from the ground forming a net of vegetation slowing me down. For a moment I was close to panic. It was as if the sweat was being wrung out of my pores, and the air pressed from my lungs. Walking became more and more difficult. I knew travel on this terrain with the Honda would have been impossible.

The machete was thrust before me to clear a narrow path every step of the way, until the steel edge would no longer cut the brush. My arm grew weary, and the surrounding plant life hardly bowed to the command of the metallic weight of the blade.

I sat down to file the dulled edge of the machete into a new sharpness and to give my tired arm a rest.

How am I going to be able to keep this up?

As if on cue, I got up and moved onward down the trail.

Ha. The Trail of life?

One good note: I was still going in a south-easterly direction.

The skyscraper-like trees gradually became lower, and the thickness of the brush thinned out until there was a large clearing nearly devoid of trees. It was filled with a thick patch of tall overhanging grass – taller than I. Almost instantly, I was out from under protecting canopy of trees and into the thick grass; my head raised to the sky. The blazing tropical sun pierced my eyes and shattered my thoughts. I was momentarily confused.

For an instant, my hopes lifted, thinking this could be an opening to another well-traveled trail; even though I was punching through the high, thin-bladed grass in a state of near panic. It was eight feet tall, thick as Kentucky blue, and brown by the constant sun. I lost whatever semblance of a trail I might have been following. There was nothing but grass. Not even the slightest sign of a path was visible.

I was lost; hopelessly caught in a motionless maze of giant green leaves, and going nowhere. For the first time, real fear took command of each hasty thought and every awkward movement. I jogged about in small frenzied circles, hoping to catch a glimpse of a trail, any trail that would lead me away from this mess. The resounding theme of the desperado dying in the clutches of a forbidden land kept pounding through my head like the vibrations of a Japanese *taiko* drum. Breathing came in quick and uneven gasps. The steady buzzing of mosquitoes, flies, cicadas in a feverish high pitch became unbearable. Large drops of sweat etched down my forehead, foraging through the thick layers of dust and pollen on my skin. Distorted green-brown vegetation moved about me in a hazy swirling motion. I felt nauseous. The tiny particles of dead grass filled my nostrils and blurred my vision, as I bulldozed about without direction.

Nearly blinded by fear and dust particles, I forced my way through the thick grass toward the apparent security of a distant treetop seen a hundred yards ahead of me. It was this savage burst of fear-driven energy that carried me out of the clutches of the tall grass and into the jungle trees once again.

But the first few steps into the trees carried me out of the grass and straight into the silky trap of a giant spider web tightly stretched between two close growing trees. The strength of the neatly spun threads stopped me immediately as if caught in the squares of a fisherman's net. I was held stationary for a few fleeting moments. One of the sticky strands of webbing crossed over my eyelid and held it shut. I looked up with my left eye and saw a dark spider, the size of my fist, running down, then up. With surprising reflexes, I spun the machete overhead and aimed for the shiny spot on its back. But I missed, and only the swooshing sound of the passing machete was heard.

The carrying weight of the machete pulled half of the spider web down around my knees, and the spider quickly disappeared up the remaining web and out of sight into the tree. I back-stepped away from the sticky trap and ran once again into the thicket.

This excitement was too much for one day. I wanted to get out, and now! I was completely lost; without a clue of where I was or where I was going.

Is this beginning to sound like a familiar theme?

Making myself stop, I sat down leaning against the cocoon of a Banyan tree trunk and breathed deeply. It was obvious I needed to gain control of myself or I would shortly perish into the bowels of the jungle. I unburdened myself from the cutting straps of the saddle-bags and sleeping roll, and took a long slow drink of water from the acidic-tasting canteen. And, reminded by a grumbling stomach, I methodically opened a can of pork-patty C-rations with the trusty P-38 for some badly needed energy.

Sitting on the soft, moist ground in the crevice of the Banyan eating the greasy pork, I began thinking enjoyable and fun thoughts and began reflecting on my nights in the hotel in Panama City.

It was an airy building with wide wooden stairwells and big rooms, but in dire need of paint and repairs. I met her the first night there, and was immediately attracted to her – and she to me. She was short and slightly built, but had the biggest, roundest, brownest eyes I had ever seen. Her name was Maria.

She approached me first, and asked where I was from. "Room 314", I had said, instead of Estados Unidos, as she had expected. We laughed, and the ice was broken. We talked for half an hour, and between her broken

English and my painful Spanish, we communicated well. She gave me little personal information except to say she was not married.

She abruptly ended the conversation at eleven PM, and I returned to my room for a hoped for restful sleep. At around two o'clock AM a light persistent tap at my door woke me. The sounds of the bustling street below and the blinking neon lights were subdued in anticipation of the new day. Who was knocking on my door at two in the morning in Panama City?

The knocking persisted, so I switched on the table lamp, raised my naked body out of the big springy bed, and slipped on my shorts and T-shirt. With the chain-lock in place, I cautiously opened the door, peaked out, and asked who was there.

"It is me. Maria."

My heart fluttered and I felt light-headed. I could hardly believe my luck as she confidently walked in. Yet there she was standing in the dim light by the table lamp.

We came together immediately. I kissed her around the ears and cheeks, and then full on the lips; at the same time pulling her onto the thin mattress. I had her nearly undressed when she suddenly sat up in bed and calmly asked for five American dollars. These words sent my once soaring ego into an instantaneous nose-dive leaving me unable to express myself.

She was a whore, a common prostitute! I had fallen for the oldest trick in the book; while believing she was actually interested in <u>me</u>. How dumb could I get?

<u>My naivety was again bursting at the seams.</u>

She waited until I was fully aroused before playing her game. I tried to make a deal with her to wait for the money until we were finished, but she was too seasoned for that. The money had to come first, or she would refuse.

I fumbled through my pants pocket until an old Abe Lincoln showed up; and I gave it to her. With the deal done, I decided to get my money's worth

and enjoyed every position, every motion, every sensuous trick I knew for mutual satisfaction – and got my $5 worth. What a night!

The next morning I received yet another shock. Maria was gone, of course, but on the night-stand was a penciled note with "Thank you" printed in English, and the five dollars on top. Nothing could be sweeter.

To add to the delight, Maria returned the next night exactly at two o'clock, and did so every night for the remainder of my week at the hotel. She never again asked for another Honest Abe.

*   *   *   *   *

Eyes closed, I was still sensing the aroma of those nights and Maria's soft skin next to mine when the fantasy was broken by the stinging bites of insects – mosquitoes, ants, and others I couldn't identify. With the sudden shock of reality at hand, the problems of how to get back to civilization broke into my mind. The agitation having subsided, I tried to calculate logically the situation by spelling everything out to myself.

There was enough food in the saddle-bags for probably a week – maybe more if I was careful – and nearly a full canteen of water. To sleep, the hammock was strong and kept me off the jungle floor at night. I had matches for a fire, a map and a compass, and at least two months before the beginning of the rainy season.

I spread the map on a smooth area for a critique of the immediate area. Both the Rio Silugandi and the Rio Playita ran parallel and were tributaries to the mother Bayano. To arrive at the Playita, Bayano, or both, I merely had to follow a generally easterly course, and it would be impossible for me to *not* get there. From the map, it appeared as if each of these rivers was within a few hours walking distance from where I guessed was my position. Once at either of these spots, I could walk to my goal – the village of Boca Playita – by following the river banks.

I started walking again, following an easterly course with the compass in one hand and the machete in the other.

Ascending the rugged hills, I went from knoll to knoll where the denseness of the jungle bush was more sporadic and varied; and the machete necessary only to slice a few snarling vines or intimidating branches. I saw a couple of brightly colored, large-beaked birds (probably macaws) to remind me I was *really* in the jungle. After seeing green and red beauties, it seemed as if I began to notice even more of them as I moved onward.

This unorthodox course of chopping, reading the compass, chopping and reading the compass continued for several hours. I was beginning to doubt the accuracy of the map; only a 1:500,000 map that was the best guesstimate between the American and Panamanian officials at the time.

Unfortunately the trail led downhill again into a swampy area. I soon discovered the swamp type of terrain is only one of two types – the other being the thick, hilly brush.

I walked into the foot-deep, black water of the swamp and continued to follow a northeasterly direction. The water was stagnant and dank, and very difficult to walk through. The putrid smell of decaying vegetation hung in the air like the invisible hydrogen sulfide of a garbage dump back home. I sloshed through the murky water for a hundred yards at a time; thinking about the motorcycle and noting the probability of dragging the Honda over the past few miles would have been nil.

To my right I noticed a steep hill with the sun breaking through the roof of trees. At the very top – to my surprise – I could see a few sunlit banana trees standing alone, as if an oasis. With rising spirits, and my stomach on empty, I scampered up the hill and soon found myself standing in the middle of a small orchard of banana trees. What an impressive sight! The fruit-bearing trees bent by the weight of the firmly bunched fruit. The wide leaves shaded them in a crown of umbrella palms.

Though most of the bananas were hard and green, and impossible to peel, I rummaged around until I found a few bunches of reddish-yellow ones hanging from a broken stem. I munched and munched until my stomach was bloated and I could eat no more. I gave little notice to the fact that these bananas tasted different from those I had eaten in the United States or during my travels through Central and South America.

I learned that particular type of banana was a plantino, or plantain – delicious when cut into thin slices and deep fried. The Latin version of potato chips.

After gorging myself, and ready to sit down to let the food digest, I saw I was standing on a narrow trail leading down the hill in the opposite direction from the swamp.

Immediately I sensed my watery goal was near, and I hustled down the newly found path with a slight case of indigestion; bananas in my pockets jabbing at my thighs. But there it was in front of me: and, judging by the great width, it had to be the Bayano River. In triumphant glee, I shouted with joy and raised my fist at the brown slippery water – its muddy banks lined with ancient gray logs. Twice as wide as the Silugandi and gleaming like the skin of some prehistoric animal, it moved majestically from my left to my right.

I had really made it!

Admittedly not much in the annals of exploration as compared to, say, Sir Richard Burton in his search for the source of the Nile River, but a great personal achievement.

The mere fact of surviving and arriving at a pre-designated spot in the jungle, and without a guide, filled me with confidence and hope.

I stepped over several logs to the water's edge and splashed the cool liquid onto my sweaty face and neck. I thought about jumping in for a bath, but concerns about my position dominated all other desires. In which direction do I walk: upstream or downstream? Was I <u>above</u> the Rio Playita and the village of Boca Playita or <u>below</u> that fork in the river; having crossed several large streams <u>after</u> leaving the Honda motorcycle at the Silugandi? For all I knew, any one of those streams could have been the Rio Playita.

*   *   *   *   *

In less than fifteen minutes, the serenity of sitting on a log by the water was broken by a faraway humming sound. It was slight at first, like the distant drone of an airplane; but getting louder. As the sound increased, I grew more tense. Then I saw it! The noise was coming from a long dark canoe, powered by an outboard motor rounding the downstream bend to my right.

I could hardly believe my luck. With so many variables and everything so relative, it seemed like a near impossibility to encounter a canoe at this exact time and spot, and after being there for such a short while.

Or <u>was</u> it luck? The canoe was full of Indians and they were heading my way. Were they friendly or hostile? Would they stop for me even if they <u>did</u> see me?

As they neared, I began wildly jumping up and down, waving my arms overhead and yelling: "YO! YO! YO!" as loud as I could. They must have thought me crazy, but this method proved effective as they quickly veered the boat from the middle of the river toward me. They were the first human beings I'd seen in nearly a week.

As the canoe drew closer, I became shy and not at all certain how to receive these Indians or how they would receive me. My mind was filled with ancient rumors of head-hunting savages with sharp spears and poisoned arrows. My feelings fluctuated from an immoveable fear to stimulating adventure – adventure of the unknown. The *unknown* often did that to me.

I decided to stand my ground and be in the moment; observing them closely. Their canoe, or *piraqua* as they are known, was the first of its kind I'd ever seen – and it was impressive! Of one straight piece of hollowed timber nearly thirty feet long, it was only the width of a man's shoulders.

This *piraqua* appeared to be extremely overloaded, with only several inches of freeboard showing above the water level. It contained three well-developed men, two bare-breasted women, four naked children and a very skinny dog, in addition to a load of personal belongings piled together near the middle of the craft. What was strikingly odd about this primitive canoe was the shiny, sleek, fifteen horse-power outboard motor clamped to the right side of the stern. It was like two different worlds!

As the canoe came to rest on the muddy bank the hunger for human contact soon overcame my wild thoughts and strange feelings. They were *Cuna* Indians, and the only indigenous people of the Darien Jungle.

The helmsman, who I assumed was also their leader, tied the canoe to a nearby log and ran without hesitation to meet me. The perfection and beauty of his young body - probably in his early twenties - was astounding; as I momentarily analyzed this radiating figure standing before me. His smooth velvety skin of shining olive-tan was without scars or blemish and seemed to glow with health and purity. Coal-black hair, cut in crock-style, fell straight from the top of his head and matched his eyes, which had the same depth and color. A simple gold ring hung from his right ear as if it were a symbol of aesthetic wealth. When smiling, his wide, full lips showed white teeth; slightly tarnished. The skin, the hair, the earring – everything about him – produced an image of a man at ease in his environment. Only the narrow band of faded man-made cloth that wrapped around his hips and straddled his legs offset the natural look of his appearance.

Modulating his first statement for emphasis in his native Cuna language, he spoke in words completely unknown to me. Perceiving my perplexed facial expressions, he easily switched to speaking in Spanish in low, well-enunciated words. Responding in halting Spanish, I tried communicating my attempt to get to Boca Playita for transportation downriver to La Capitanna, and then to Chepo for the return trip to Panama City. To prevent the confusion that comes with the language barrier, I decided against telling him about the dead motorcycle lying on the bank by the Rio Silugandi.

Once my purpose was understood, his friendliness and willingness to help became apparent; though I doubt he ever understood why I was at that spot by the river where he "found" me. *"Si, Si."* he repeated several times, and waved me toward the *piraqua*. He would transport me to the Playita – only a short distance upstream and along his route. As best as I could understand, he was going to a place many miles up the Bayano

River to a place whose name I didn't understand and could not find on the map.

The leader quickly and forcefully cleared a seat for me just in front of the pile of personal things; several aluminum pots, a stem of bananas, and what looked like a bag of beans or rice. The others stared intently in profound amazement. I wedged my way into the small space allotted to me, and the canoe quickly headed upstream with a disquieting roar of the outboard.

It was a new and exciting adventure to be seated in such a narrow canoe full of Indians heading upstream on a river in the jungle. WOW! The slightest movement of my body to one side or the other would surely tip the *piraqua* over and drop us all into the mud-stained waters of the Bayano River. And who knew how deep it was or what kind of strange fish it contained? But who cared? For the first time since entering the jungle the feeling of freedom once again raced through my mind and body. For now, the vice-like grip of the enclosing forest was gone, replaced with the cool wind rushing past my face, fluffing my hair, and filling my shirt like a balloon. The healthy rays of the sun reflected off the soft river water onto my face while the mesmerizing blue of the sky fixed my attention on the horizon.

Few words were passed between the Cuna. The children, 3 boys and a girl stared at me for long periods of time and often giggled. The women avoided eye contact as I disciplined my gaze, sometimes unsuccessfully, from glancing at their breasts. The leader was at the helm of the outboard and the other two held long poles on either side. It was probably two families returning to their chosen spot in the jungle away from the madness of encroaching civilization.

The roaring of the engine didn't last long, as the mighty Bayano turned into shallow rapids causing the driver to stop the motor. The men smoothly jumped into the water and began pushing the canoe over the rapids and slippery rocks on the bottom. As a display of friendship and appreciation I removed my boots and socks, rolled up my trousers, and popped into the chilly water to help in the push over the rapids. At first the hosts seemed upset that their guest should have to work and wanted me to remain seated. But soon they became accustomed to my help and accepted it with grace. Only the skinny dog seemed excited and meekly barked at the constant movement of leaps in and out of the water.

Off and on, each family member would stare at me in apparent perplexed examination – looking, searching, for some mutual identity. Sometimes the Cuna women laughed at me; probably wondering how anyone could appear so debauched in their simple jungle habitat. My mangy red beard and long ratty blonde hair seemed to be an attention getter. While their bodies were naked or near-naked, my clothes were dirty, torn, and ragged and covered nearly every part of my body. And why wear a hat? But why a person unaccustomed to the often harsh elements of nature would expose himself to the demands of the jungle to the point of exhaustion was, I'm sure, beyond their willingness to comprehend.

Yet through their peering eyes there seemed to be a sense of trepidation that –though I was in need of their immediate assistance – I somehow had the power to eventually expose them to the unknown world of the "outside"; that I would quickly gather them all together and fly them away to some strange land on a magic carpet easily extracted from my saddle bags. Their world was a sacred realm where basic truths and integrity existed without question; self-sufficiency and independence reigned supreme; their customs and culture perpetuated. Still, they maintained a certain curiosity about me, my life, and my culture that almost forced them to know more; and the same for me about them.

After about an hour of travel, I saw a lone *piraqua* resting on the riverbank several hundred yards upstream to my left. I guessed Boca Playita was nearby. With a loud voice beaming with confidence the driver notified everyone (but especially for me) the fork in the river just ahead was the Rio Playita. He smoothly guided the *piraqua* toward the riverbank and rested it in the soft mud.

I had this urge to go with them. To say: "Take me with you." I'm standing in ankle deep water, my boots slung over the saddle bags on my back. So what do I do? Ask to go along and live with them, or do my own thing?

I walked ashore and unloaded my gear on a nearby rock, and said nothing.

Before I could offer money or a personal gift, the canoe was once again plowing upstream. A poignant *adios* was exchanged between us, and the canoe propelled around the bend and out of sight. I would never see them again.

The whole experience of getting to the banks of the Bayano, being picked up by the Cuna in a *piraqua*, and transported to the mouth of the Rio Playita was surreal.

*   *   *   *   *

I pulled out the map to be certain of my position. The village of Boca Playita, according to this map, should be on the opposite bank of the Rio Playita from where I stood. Surveying the area around the forked river, I saw no people or anything representing a community; only the empty *piraqua* several hundred yards down the Bayano jutting out from the shore.

To be certain there was no village away from the bank of the Playita on the opposite side, I took off my boots and stripped down to my underwear and swam across. At the spot where I landed, a high wall of mud prevented me from looking around for the mysterious village so I swam another forty or fifty yards around a bend and soon found footage and climbed to the top of the muddy wall. I found two huts with half of the thatched roofs missing and no people.

So, the map was wrong! Why would a village be placed on a map where none existed? I was flabbergasted and discouraged and could see from this vantage point the entire Bayano-Playita basin was without habitation.

Swimming back to my equipment, I momentarily stood near the water's edge drying myself in the thick tropical air and warm late afternoon sun.

Suddenly a deep beckoning voice broke the evening stillness drawing my eyes to the lone canoe downstream. Turning, I saw a brightly dressed, dark-skinned Indian standing beside the *piraqua* over a hundred yards away. In the excited search for the elusive Boca Playita the *piraqua* was nearly forgotten.

After dressing, I trudged along the bank of rocks, mud, and dead tree branches until I met face-to-face with this fully dressed Cuna. He appeared to be of a different tribe than the *piraqua* Indians but maintained the same stature of independent nobility. The ageless steel gray eyes of this tall man were the first things I noticed about him. He was older, probably in his late fifties. He wore a flaming blue long-sleeved shirt which contrasted sharply with his soiled green pants hanging loosely at the ankles. His bare feet, like his face, showed the wrinkles won by the experiences of time. A black derby-like hat with a small yellow feather rested flamboyantly to one side of his head; giving the impression of originality without eccentricity.

A quick rapport built between us as he began a chain of questions in slow determined Spanish. One perplexing question he asked over and over was: "*¿Usted Perú?*" "NO" I repeated. "*Soy de Estados Unidos.*" I am from the United States. As best I could understand, he said his name was *"Arkar"*. The high level of intensity and involvement of our conversation continued until he asked me to write on a piece of paper my name and address for him to keep. He was intent on learning the pronunciations of words in English. Neither of us knew many words of Spanish but the words each of us knew were usually the same. We communicated famously, and for the moment enjoyed each others company.

Our conversation was temporarily broken by the shocking appearance of his son. And what a shock it was! I could hardly believe my eyes – he was an *albino*. I had heard in Panama City the Cuna Indians have one of the largest - if not the largest - incident rates of albinos of any sect or group in the world. But this fact was not fully driven home until the tiny boy of nine or ten years old came running down the hill to be with his father. His bleached white skin was severely marred by large blotches of red skin over his thin legs and bare buttocks. A small head of thin yellow hair hung down his gaunt face. The squinting of his pink-rimmed eyes made it impossible for me to distinguish any color in them. Against the raw jungle world he seemed so frail, even helpless. I felt sorry for him and instinctively wanted to do something to help him. But how could *I* help *him*?

His nearly clenched eyelids only peered up at me with a continuous questioning expression, never once straying, as if asking: "Who are you?" Perhaps I was the first "outsider", or Caucasian with skin nearly the same, the boy had ever seen. Did he think we were brothers, or somehow related? I didn't know, and because of the frustrating language barrier I'll never know. But the penetrating glare of his eyes contained the persistence of hope.

Visually retracing the boys' footsteps to the top of the riverbank, I received yet another jolt. There, standing close together and looking down at me with a curious interest were two *female* albinos; sisters of the boy next to me. They looked like twins. They were the same height and skin coloration (or discoloration) as the boy – their brother I presumed. Perhaps the most striking feature of their appearance was their hair. Though yellow like the boy's, it was closely cut in a short "butch" style.

For a minute there, I thought I was hallucinating; having double vision. This whole scene is very unreal.

And, whereas the boy wore nothing, the girls were clothed in toga style skirts and wrap-around blouses to cover their shoulders.

Incredibly, the front part of their tops were made from "molas". Molas are an incredibly beautiful and colorful textile art-form depicting jungle life; especially the wildlife. It is a technique of appliqué and reverse appliqué sewn by hand with stitches that are not visible, or barely visible. Had I known then what I know now... I would surely have traded for, or bought, several molas.

Whatever is on the front of their blouses looks pretty neat. I wonder if the color red or the design means anything. It kind of looks like chickens or birds to me.

Their lower legs and lower arms were covered with laced bracelets of kaleidoscopic colors, causing their skin to puff over the bottom rings.

They just stared at me, and I at them.

Ironically, neither the sisters nor the boy spoke one word to me or their father during the entire time. The whole family presented a rather motley picture: the father, wife and eldest son (both of whom I met later) were of normal dark brown skin, but the twins and youngest son were albinos.

Wow! What are the odds of anyone having 3 out of 4 children be albinos?

Later, I learned Arkar was an important, but maverick chief who roamed the jungle nomadically with his family.

Arkar made me an offering of bananas and oranges, and I continued our enlightening conversation, pausing only to swallow the half-chewed fruit. In return for the fruit, I gave him the gift of a single fish hook and three of the twenty-two caliber bullets out of the box I carried from Panama City. He was overjoyed when I handed him these gifts, especially at the sight of the shiny twenty-twos, and immediately asked me to stay the night in the extra hut – visible from where we stood across the river. At first it seemed strange that he would ask me to stay in the hut across the river, but I learned it was customary for Cuna to never permit strangers, especially foreigners, to spend the night in their homes.

Despite the uneasy feelings, I accepted the offer and he smoothly pushed the two of us across the river in his *piraqua* with a long wooden pole. He showed me the old, but solidly built hut, and departed without a word, leaving me to hang my hammock and build a fire in the shadows of the onrushing night.

But instead of being comforted by the light of the fire and the knowledge of nearby humans, a growing sense of uneasiness crept over me like a stifling fog. I didn't know why.

It could be that I really don't trust anyone or anything except myself. This reminds me of the recurring nightmare I began having when I was nine or ten. I am alone at night in bed – Mom, Pete, and Sheila are not home. From my bed I hear someone creeping up the squeaky stairs as my eyes fixate on the light switch by the doorway with a door. The squeaking stops and I know someone is standing at the top of the stairs. Suddenly I see a single, dark, gloved hand slowly inching its way around the corner of the doorway toward the light switch. I can see the muscles flexing on the hand inside the leather glove. I am frozen; cannot move or scream. I am certain the person connected to the hand is coming after me to smother or kill me. How can I escape? Where can I go? What can I do? That mental image of the hand in a dark leather glove slowly moving toward the light switch still scares the hell out of me.

Coincidentally, a strange incident did happen that night. I was sleeping lightly in the hammock when – THUMP – I was suddenly awakened by the shock of finding myself on the hard ground. Dazed and disoriented, I looked around and could see by the ambers of the fire I was on the ground, but not knowing how I got there. Thinking someone – "they" – were coming to get me, I jumped up and grabbed the wet handle of the machete, ready to defend myself and began stabbing in the darkness around me. But there was no one – no "they" coming for me. After regaining some of my sense and checking the ropes I discovered the knot I tied at the foot of the hammock had slipped from the condensation of the river-bottom air, and my weight caused it and me to fall to the ground.

*   *   *   *   *

In the morning I was greeted by Arkar and his white-skinned son with an offering of more bananas and oranges, <u>and</u> a request for six more twenty-two bullets. I momentarily hesitated because the bullets were a valuable commodity in the jungle, as I came to realize, and could be used to bargain for just about anything. The box initially contained fifty of the tiny twenty-two projectiles. With three already gone and a request for six more, forty-one would be left. And with an uncertain future, each twenty-two could weigh heavily on the eventual outcome of my jungle journey; and the motorcycle could still be retrieved. Arkar was aware he held the upper hand, so I submitted to his request – but not without the feeling of being "conned".

So what? No big deal! I know this guy is taking advantage of me, but hey, I like him and wish I could spend a couple of months with him. And besides, he has a family and probably needs them more than I do.

About an hour later, Arkar hailed a small *piraqua* with a young Cuna and his spouse heading downstream carrying, what looked like, their worldly belongings on their canoe. He called in an authoritative chiefly voice that carried across the quiet river basin and into the thickness of the stilled jungle. The sun was just coming into view. A slight breeze was barely noticeable, and the river was smooth as glass. Except for the occasional sound of a mating bird, all was quiet – almost dream-like.

The young Indian replied to Arkar in the same strong monotone voice with obvious agreement, as his voice too carried across the waters of the Rio Bayano and into the woods. The conversation was unintelligible to me but pleasing to the ears.

The young man effortlessly steered his *piraqua* to us. Through the confusion that always happens with hasty departures, I guessed the young Cuna was to transport me downstream. To where, I didn't understand.

And who cares? I don't have a clue where I'm going. But I trust them. And besides, it's all part of the grand adventure.

Yet I felt confident he would lead me to a village or some community.

My gear was stowed among the pile of food and kitchen utilities, and I settled into the only spot available, with my chin resting on my knees. As the canoe inched away from the bank and started downstream, I turned my head to watch Arkar and his son; a memorable picture still etched in my mind.

*   *   *   *   *

This *piraqua* was much smaller (about twenty feet in length) and without an outboard motor, but with a distracting bare-breasted woman. The young Cuna moved the boat along by the use of a long wooden pole. What a pleasure it was to watch the great human specimen of nature perform the art of poling this hand-crafted boat over the smooth or rough river waters! He executed each movement from the forward tip of the canoe with the agility of a ballet dancer, causing the bow of the boat to rise like a sailboat catching a fresh wind. From the stern of the boat I watched in jealous admiration, wanting to try it myself.

At first glance, the movements looked easy. But when scrutinizing the whole procedure, I noticed that each movement required the greatest amount of stability, strength, stamina, and timing. First, the Cuna placed the long pole slightly forward of the moving boat and jammed the pole into the river bottom. He would then gracefully turn about facing the back of the boat and walk several steps while pushing downward with an even power. He then returned to the bow of the boat and started again. The width of the bow sprit at the front of the boat where the poling was done could not have been more than ten inches, and occasionally became wet from splashing waters or water dripping from the pole. This made the walking up and down while pushing on the pole precariously slippery as the *piraqua* wash pushed forward in a soft, slow, motion.

His wife, whom I could see only with a difficult twisting of my neck, sat at the stern and acted as helmsman steering the boat with a long-handled, thin, wooden paddle. Neither spoke a word to the other during my time with them.

As we moved slowly down the Bayano River, the early morning sun rose higher overhead, and encouraged by a balmy current of air massaging my face, I went in and out of a state of drowsiness. My thoughts bounced lightly from the intriguing jungle around me to dream-like fantasies in my mind. Occasionally during this state of semi-consciousness, I raised my burning eyelids to watch the rhythmic movements of the youthful captain, sure-footed, perfect timing, fully focused on moving his destiny forward.

Like the movements in a slow-motion movie, we silently stroked our way over the soft surface of the warm water, faintly disturbing the reflecting impressions of the overhanging trees and the white puffy clouds to look like a living Monet or Degas. The vibrant skin on the back of the Cuna was dotted with pellets of sweat magnifying his well-toned muscles that hardened with each pull of the pole; groomed and conditioned into full maturity from early childhood.

Ya know, I could really get to like this. Learn to live off of what the jungle has to offer, get a boat like this...

More frequently my daydreams were scattered by verbal greetings offered between our driver and various Indian families living along the banks of the river. Most were groups forced from their mountain homes by the winter droughts, like many of the animals, to the Bayano River for the greater abundance of food and water.

Rounding a wide bend in the river, we came to a larger grouping of bamboo huts roosting on the high river bank. Many *piraquas* stretched out from the bank like thin cigars. Our boat turned toward the look-alike canoes and I began to understand this was the end of my journey with this Cuna and his wife – who I could now see was pregnant.

Where the village was located on the map or what its name was I did not know. Giving the Cuna two American dollars for the excursion, I collected my gear and walked to the top of the river bank. Along with the many huts, the village contained two large _congressos_, or community meeting halls where tribal decisions are made.

I was momentarily stunned when, at the far end of the village, I saw a house. A real house! It was a wooden frame structure built on stilts, and it stuck out like a sore thumb. The white paint was still bright and the tin roof seemed impressive – but would have fit better into a small suburban stateside town than in the mist of a jungle. I just stood there in amazement for several minutes. Finally, a passing male Cuna told me it was a missionary and encouraged me to go there.

I hurried to the stairs leading up to the doorway and gently knocked. Mr. and Mrs. Dave Wilson introduced themselves and their two daughters, aged eight and ten. The village was Maje, and the Wilson's were American missionaries (Baptist, I believe) who had penetrated the jungle in an attempt to convert the Indians to Christianity. They all seemed somewhat bewildered by my appearance but accepted me with open arms.

The light colored jacket I wore for protection against the harshness of the jungle brush had turned many shades of brown and black from the strain of the journey thus far. My straw hat had slowly disintegrated and was full of torn holes. I was filthy dirty and my hair was sticky with grease. Their eyes told me they knew saddle-bags were not exactly an ideal rucksack for carrying jungle supplies. I felt ashamed of my appearance and for what I had to confess about the forsaken motorcycle and my experiences in the jungle thus far. But after relating the story, Mr. Wilson told me to go down to a secluded spot in the river for a good bath, and dinner would be ready by the time I finished.

I walked down the bank to a quiet spot along the river's edge and began to undress. It was not until I took off my Levi's and boots that I saw, in stunned disbelief, the lower half of my body was covered with a multitude of brown and red spots – some the size of pinheads, others larger. It was as if the skin on my legs had been *spritzed* with a dark soda pop, except these spots could not be washed off. After the initial shock I realized they were parasitic ticks, chiggers, and red bugs all concentrated in the warm areas of my lower body sucking blood. I never felt them penetrating my skin; the ticks were by far the worst and most abundant of all.

Laboriously, I began picking and scraping them off one by one. And, not being satisfied with just picking them off, I needed to kill them by popping their shelled bodies between my fingernails and flicking them into the river knowing they would never again enter the skin of another human being. Their brittle outer shell was no match for my hardened fingernails as the blood, my blood, squirted out of their body onto my hands. Soon my fingers were covered with the tiny shell bits and darkened blood. It was in vain that I tried to squeeze out the chiggers. So I lit a cigarette and successfully burned out many of them. I picked, scratched, and clawed at my ankles, behind my knees, and crotch area until I felt satisfied my body was, for now, cleansed of these lecherous insects.

After scrubbing my body with soap I stood drying in the still jungle air, hoping the healthy rays from the setting sun would help heal the insect bites. Although I washed off the dirt and blood I continued to feel unclean, as if my body was still crawling with invisible insects. Despite the tranquility of the surroundings, I imagined them sucking away at my blood until exploding from gluttony. Everything I touched seemed dirty. Everything I saw seemed harmful. Everything I heard sounded like part of the conspiracy. I wanted to shed my skin, scrub my brain and fly to a world of sterile existence free from dirt, darkness, and disease, where living was effortless.

Instead, I returned to the Missionary and joined the Wilson family for dinner.

*   *   *   *   *

I enjoyed my first hot meat since leaving Panama City. The soup, steamed rice and stew were tantalizingly delicious – but hot. After the second mouth full the taste buds on my tongue were burnt and the remaining food – though satisfying to my stomach – remained tasteless. The after-meal conversation was candid and enlightening. And, because it was my first English discussion in a long time, I easily dominated by going into minute details about the long struggle with the motorcycle and the consequent walk to the Bayano River.

Dave, as I came to know him, displayed a fluent ability to speak both the Spanish and Cuna languages and had a wealth of knowledge of the Indian culture. He shared much about the religious beliefs, tribal customs, and living habits of the Cuna Indians. Their dialect, he said, made it easier for them to understand English than Spanish. This explains why the conversations with Arkas and the young man in our *piraqua* were relatively easy and enjoyable.

When asked about the friendliness of the Cuna toward foreigners, Dave likened their attitude, in many ways, as similar to the way the *American* Indians resented the U.S. government for many reasons. Like the American Indians, the Cuna were being methodically pushed further and further back into the interior until forced onto reservations. Their area of sovereign land keeps growing smaller and smaller and, as the area of land shrinks, their animosity toward the Panamanian government grows proportionately. And, because of their strong desire to be free and independent, they had no recourse but to resist. But an obvious foreigner like me was treated with respect and courtesy, as is their habit.

It was here that I learned about a guy named "Peru" from South American, who went traipsing around the Darien in an attempt to unify the Cuna into a political force. This explained why Arkas persistently called me "Peru". He wasn't asking if I had been to the country of Peru, but if I had seen him.

The Mission itself was very ill-equipped and restrained by the shrinking funds received quarterly from their home organization in the U.S. as a result of five or six missionaries being speared to death by Indians in the Ecuador part of the Amazon basin in 1956 or so.

Being sparse and frugal, the building wasn't exactly designed as a resting place for wayward jungle novices like me. This made it necessary to string my hammock in the living room because it was only a three-room building. I spent the early hours of the first night reading books and periodicals, and was afforded the luxury of sleeping without the bothersome mosquito-net drooping over my head.

However, that first night of attempting to sleep, I received the initial symptoms of a horror that was to plague me for my remaining days in the Darien Jungle: the after-shock of the insect bites. The bites I had sustained eventually became infected and inflamed causing a slow wave of agonizing itching of my skin around the bitten areas; particularly in my calves. The itching would build to a peak and then a sudden shock wave would drive through my nervous system with a jolt and the speed of electricity; but only after the scratching resulted in blood under my fingernails and fingertips. It was an endless cycle of scratching followed by the electric shock waves. I scratched until even the muscles in my hands and forearms tired. Eventually, the itching stopped.

Then, and without warning, the cycle returned, tearing me from a modicum of sleep. Eventually, at the end of a cycle of itching and scratching, I began losing the desire for the much needed sleep because of the anticipation of a rude awakening by the sudden attacks. I slept very little, if at all, that first night.

The next day I told Mr. & Mrs. Wilson of my desire to attempt a retrieval of the Honda motorcycle. Immediately, Dave went in search of an available Cuna and a *piraqua* for hire. No more than thirty minutes later, he returned with the same Cuna (by the name Egwa) who had transported me to Maje. Egwa was the only person willing and able to abandon the chores of working the banana trees for a day; *his* primary reason for coming to Maje during the dry season. Each working day was worth to him the equivalent of two dollars and fifty cents. In our negotiations he requested five dollars for his time, labor, and use of the canoe. This price was high, but…

Again, here I am stuck in a position without a choice. Man, I hate that.

We quickly boarded the *piraqua* and were soon on our way up the Bayano seeking the mouth of the Rio Silugandi.

Without his wife, I became the helmsman at the stern of the boat. At first, the sharply pointed paddle made a difficult rudder to use against the strong downward rush of the powerful Bayano River. But after a few miles of bumbling with it, steering the boat upstream became a pleasure. In the backwaters I assisted in our efforts to move upstream by paddling. In the shallow waters when the bottom of the boat scraped the rocks I lent a hand by jumping in the river and helping with the chore of pushing the *piraqua* to deeper water.

The weight of the water against the wooden paddle flexed the muscles in my arms and back. The exercise was stimulating. Soon I removed my shirt. Occasionally an overhanging vine ruffled my hair or a leaf would fall against my chest as my eyes followed it floating in the moving water. I felt primitive, yet somehow in tune with nature. And for a short time I again entertained the idea of living in the jungle, as a primitive or "natural" man. But this fantasy was easily discounted after hours of slow; upstream moving became tiresome and boring.

I steered the canoe on the left bank of the river within a few feet of the jungle for easy poling and shade. Finally the mouth of the Rio Silugandi was sighted, and the canoe was slowly maneuvered to the left. Once "inside" the waters of the Suligandi I was reminded of the more pristine beauty of the jungle. From the comfort of the boat it was like a Hollywood nature film where the water showed the purity of a virgin spring. Compared to the murky Rio Bayano, lens-like clarity of the water displayed schools of darting fish, fallen tree branches and sparkling pebbles. The riverbanks were the color of a young fawn. Patches of multicolored flowers burst skyward trying to reach the sun; adding their fragrances to the sweet smelling air.

But I cannot allow myself to be deceived by this romanticism! One small drop of this water in my mouth and the amoeba would deplete my body to death. Thank God I still had plenty of Halazone tablets left. One misstep and I could drown, break a leg; get bitten by a snake; or worse.

However, in contrast to the deep waters of the Bayano, the Silugandi soon became an obstacle course as the width of the river grew more and more narrow. Fallen trees were the most irritating obstacle, but very shallow rapids, boulders, and sunken tree stumps added to our difficulties.

Hours after forcing the *piraqua* up the narrowing river without locating the Honda motorcycle we became dubious of ever finding it. Of course I had no way of knowing for certain I had left the motorcycle on the banks of the Suligandi, and was beginning to doubt myself and the reliability of the map, for it had been wrong before.

As the river narrowed and became shallower, Egwa more frequently looked at me with a questioning stare.

With that look, I know this guy is asking himself <u>and</u> me: What's going on here? Are we on a wild goose chase, or what?

The sun was well past its midway point in the sky letting us know it was getting late in the afternoon. A big decision had to be made, and soon! What to do? Continue up the Suligandi or return to the missionaries at Maje? Was the motorcycle really that important? What would I do if it was never found? How would I get back to the States? And an even larger question, regardless of the motorcycle, was: would I want to continue *walking* through the jungle into Colombia

*   *   *   *   *

Soon my doubts were joined with the doubts of Egwa's and we resigned ourselves to not finding the motorcycle. We stopped the upstream effort and paused for a short while on the riverbank without speaking.

Gently and effortlessly we began gliding downstream. Once on the Bayano, the ride to Maje was peaceful and pleasant in the early evening sunlight. Egwa looked as if he had mastered the art of disappointment, whereas I was long-faced as we neared Maje.

<u>Sometimes I still believe the motorcycle was found. In the original manuscript I wrote a scenario where it was found because my personal sense of shame had not yet been overcome, and it still surfaces occasionally – like an alcoholic in relapse. I had been raised in a poor Irish fatherless environment, was in prison by the age of 16, and had left a pregnant girlfriend in my early youth. My desire to outwardly "look good" was my way of hiding this inner damning shame; perhaps the most hideous of all human afflictions.</u>

A motored *piraqua* passed on the left heading upstream full of Cuna and supplies.

Shortly after my arrival, Dave and I had a long discussion lasting until the end of dinner about the pros and cons of continuing my walk into Colombia. Of course, he subtly encouraged my return to the United States by explaining how he could get me transportation downstream to Boca Canita, El Llano, or even La Capitanna, and from either one of these places it would be reasonably cheap and easy to get motorized transportation to Panama City.

The thought of another failure in life caused my emotions to override whatever reason or logic I may have possessed at the time giving myself permission to deny the overwhelming odds, bury the stifling fears of the unknown, and face the awesomeness of this challenge. The idea of returning to the United States, and especially returning to my friends in Los Angeles, without at least a partial success of getting into South America was totally deflating.

First, *could* I make it through the remainder (over two hundred miles) of the Darien Jungle into Colombia alone and on foot? Second, what would I do if and when I did get there? I had little money (a little over one hundred dollars), no contacts there and no means of getting money.

But by now I was again feeling that old feeling of the need for freedom I felt before leaving Los Angeles.

But what is freedom? Freedom without responsibility is but a temporary illusion!

Without the motorcycle I felt as if I could do anything. Now it was a different kind of shakedown cruise. Amazingly, and easily blocking out the sweaty grit, the swarms of mosquitoes, the bloody tick bites, and the intense psychic and physical exhaustion, I was getting recharged with the thrill of adventuring.

Oh, how I loved the newness of being in places I'd never been, and seeing people I'd never seen. Experiencing the sights, the sounds, the smells, the tastes combined to make me feel alive.

I had convinced myself to go to Colombia.

There, it is done! The decision is made. I'm going. After all, I'm a Capricorn. What can I say? It will be just another notch in my belt of things I've done and places I've been.

*   *   *   *   *

Seeing the stubbornness, Dave offered to help in my effort to get to Colombia. He suggested I travel by *piraqua* upstream to the village of Ipeti on the Rio Ipeti – not shown on my map. From there he heard of a trail heading in an easterly direction. Where the trail went, he did not know but assumed it would eventually lead to the Chucunaque River; one if the main arteries of the Darien Jungle that eventually drained into the Pacific Ocean. Once at the Chucunaque, he thought I could probably catch a canoe going downriver to El Real, the "capital" of the Darien. After El Real, he could only guess.

During our long conversation, Dave gently tried to persuade me against undertaking such a journey alone and with little jungle experience. He said he couldn't understand my "just for the thrill of it" attitude. Nor was I able to fully comprehend or articulate it. He concluded by saying it would be a few days before a canoe would be passing Maje and that I should think about it.

That same evening I went down by the Suligandi for a relaxing bath.

What happened next is something I purposefully left out of my notes and the original manuscript for the same shame-based reasons above, but the vividness remains. Lodging in a jungle missionary surely compounded the sense of guilt and shame to ensure the memory was permanent.

Arriving at the Suligandi River for my bath, the first thing I did was to urinate. There was a slight burning sensation, but I tried to ignore it. As I started washing my groin area, I saw puss coming out of the head of my penis.

I had the clap! I had caught a venereal disease – VD. There was no doubt about it. And there was no doubt I had gotten it from my prostitute-friend at the hotel in Panama City.

I knew it was gonorrhea because I had contracted it before while stationed on Okinawa, Japan as a paratrooper in 1961. And, needless to say, this time I was in a more critical situation.

After a short time of intense self-analysis, I knew I had to go to Dave. Unable to look him directly in the eyes, I confessed my ignoble behavior and the consequences that was VD. He looked at me with astonishment and disbelief, and asked me to show him the puss. I did, and said it had just started. He tried to be verbally non-judgmental, but was betrayed by the look on his face.

Nonetheless, he reacted swiftly by running to the house to tell his wife and daughter he was leaving immediately to go downstream and would return in the morning. To where he went, I never knew.

He returned early the next morning with some medication. Here again is another part of the story I shamefully blocked-out. I simply do not remember which type of medication he gave me. It may have been penicillin or tetracycline. But this could be just another self-made memory. I do remember he never asked for money to pay for the life-saving medication.

Whatever it was, it worked! Thank God for modern medicine, and for people willing to help someone in need.

Dave and I continued the conversations. I told him it was financially out of the question to hire a *piraqua* to carry me up the river to Ipeti. Consequently, the only option left was to wait for a canoe returning to Ipeti and hope they had space available and a willingness to take me along. As a passenger, he said, it would be easy to bargain for a reasonable deal.

*   *   *   *   *

The wait took several days. And, being of little patience, the time went by excruciatingly slowly.

In the mean time, I was looking for ways to work off my room and board. The Wilson's had been slowly clearing the jungle off four or five acres of land for farming behind their mission home, so I cheerfully sharpened my machete and joined in cutting and dragging everything to a central pile to be burned. The hard work satisfied my need for physical activity but did little to thwart my anxious anticipation of moving on.

The daylight hours were spent with one eye on the swinging machete slashing through the moist vegetation, and the other eye always on the river; while the nights allowed me to visualize the Cuna, the boat, the river, and the journey upstream to Ipeti. Mr. Wilson was consoling. He was familiar with the Indians there and was even thinking of building another missionary there soon. They always stopped in Maje before continuing up the Bayano, so there was little possibility of me "missing the boat".

All the while, the VD was healing.

Several canoes passed the mission but quietly continued onward without stopping. The waiting was becoming unbearable, but there was nothing I could do except keep chopping, chopping, and chopping. The calluses hardened.

Then, about mid-morning on the fourth day, while still chopping away at the vegetation in the heavy brush, Dave called from the house: "Buck, a boat for Ipeti is here!"

The date was February fifteenth, 1965. It was ten days after I'd entered the Darien Jungle and I was about to embark on the most perilous voyage of my life.

Chapter 4

T hree middle-aged Cuna, all men, were returning to Ipeti in their primitive dug-out *piraqua* with a large Evinrude outboard motor strapped onto the rear-right side. They had come from La Capitanna, near the mouth of the Bayano, where they traded bananas for necessary household goods and food staples. And, as Dave forecasted, they stopped in Maje to speak with the Cuna of Maje before continuing upstream toward their home farther toward the interior of the Darien.

After a short debate with Dave, the Indians decided to fit me into their *piraqua* and transport me to the village of Ipeti. Initially, the three men requested ten dollars for this service, but after convincing them of my rather poor financial situation, Dave was able to get the price down to seven dollars and fifty cents.

Again, my terminal naivety allowed me to enter the jungle with only nine dollars in cash (the rest in American Express Travelers checks) – never expecting to spend even half that much. I had already given seven of those dollars to Egwa (for the ride to Maje and the day-search for the Honda). This left me with only two dollars cash.

I offered the two dollars in cash, 10 twenty-two shells, and the extra machete bartered for while helping to clear Dave's farm land.

They balked, so I threw in another 10 shells.

Their eyes lit up and they happily accepted my offer.

They were leaving immediately. So I ran to the house grabbed the already packed motorcycle bags, and rushed back to the waiting canoe.

The Wilson's with their two daughters came to the river's edge. Each said goodbye and wished me luck. I told them of my gratitude and my desire to someday see them again, which we all knew would never happen.

*I still remember that identical look in the eyes of Dave and Mrs. Wilson. They probably thought of me as **crazy** – completely out of my mind! But their penetrating glare also expressed a genuine compassion and a sincere wanting the best for me. There was a sense of mutuality between us: they knew I didn't really support what they were doing with the Cuna, but I admired their strength of character; and I knew they didn't like what I was doing, yet they somehow respected my faith seen by them as the apparent lack of fear. As human beings we parted with a warm regard for one another.*

Dave's parting statement was one that haunted my memory throughout my days in the jungle, and for years after: "Don't worry about us or the mission," he said, "I only hope you find what it is you are looking for."

The canoe slipped from the soft, muddy banks at Maje and quietly powered up the Bayano. I glanced backward once; observing the Wilson's dogged trek up the riverbank toward their home and their life.

Once again I was on my way. I was in motion, and happier.

*   *   *   *   *

The remaining daylight hours were spent powering the *piraqua* up the Bayano; past the mouth of the Silugandi; past Arkar's hut, and onward. Each new bend in the river provided an unfamiliar enchantment of tropical birds, entwined foliage, and an overwhelming sense of beauty. Excitement bordered on bliss.

The river remained the only constant. Like an immutable law of the universe, the forceful current moved toward the ocean without thought, without feeling. The three Cuna and I, in a primitive dug-out canoe with a modern motor resisted this natural flow, or at least attempted to. It was men, machine, and nature. What a deal!

The farther up the Bayano we drove, the more often was it necessary for the four of us to jump out of the *piraqua* and physically push the canoe over the shallow rapids; sometimes as shallow as six inches. Our mutual drive to keep moving upward and our struggles to push the boat over the low water areas forged a feeling of kinship between us. The three men were close in age. One had an old scar running diagonally across his left forearm, about four inches long. He was the leader.

The feeling of camaraderie made the chores and wet feet of traveling in such a primitive fashion almost a pleasure. And time moved fast, until the evening dusk persuaded us to the hazards of continuing.

We stopped and set-up camp on a long sand-bar between the overhanging trees and the quieting water. After unrolling the poncho and sleeping gear, I moved around with the Cuna gathering dry wood for the night's fire. Once it was burning we sat around in a circle staring at the brightness and the flickering flames. Only an occasional exchange of a few Cuna sentences broke the meditative silence.

Just before retiring to their blankets for the night, the Indians honored me by offering me a drink of their _chicha_ – a nutritious drink of the tropics made of water and coarsely ground fermented maize.

*I say "honored" because it is only a rare occasion the people of the Cuna tribe offer a stranger their **chicha** drink, and usually as a token of outreach.*

Being fully aware of the custom and the insult of refusal, learned at the Maje missionary, I pulled the wooden stopper out of the curved elongated gourd and gulped down a healthy mouthful.

I was caught in-between again; apprehensive but honored. The apprehensiveness was about the possible serious side-effects resulting from ingesting the *chicha* made from the water directly out of the river. The river has a multitude of uses, but also functions as a primary means of human sewage disposal and for cleaning themselves afterward. However, I was more concerned with keeping the harmony with the Cuna than the dysentery side effects.

We all slept soundly by the fire on the mattress of sand by the river's side, undisturbed.

*   *   *   *   *

With only a faint tinge of gray light showing in the slice of sky along the river and between the silhouetted trees, I was gently awakened by the soft touch of the leaders' scarred arm. It was time to continue upstream.

Not a word was spoken as all the sleeping-gear was methodically rolled and placed in the canoe exactly in position as it had been the day before. But just before departing I motioned to the leader for a short delay, and rushed to the opposite end of the sand to relieve myself of urine and the already loose feces.

Thus, once again we started up the emotionless Bayano River feeling our way through the thick fog smothering the surface of the water and the nearby jungle.

Eventually the sun chased the heavy vapors and a new day had begun.

*   *   *   *   *

Still early in the morning, the canoe made a neat turn to the starboard. This was the Rio Ipeti, the leader informed me. This tributary was of the same majestic beauty as the Silugandi, except its banks of raw clean earth appeared so definite and steep it looked as though it had been cut out by a giant celestial knife. More than likely, the sharpness was caused by the raging waters of the rainy season. Some mounds, thirty or more feet high clearly displayed the layers of clay soil and thin slate, gradually tapering until fused into the water. The glass-like water in turn reflected the long lines of rock with such precision it was impossible to distinguish the beginning from the end. It was like a huge stone-age arrowhead with a trail of wavy smoke, as the piercing tip of the canoe quickly shattered the mirror images beyond recognition as we puttered upriver.

We stopped for a midday rest and for time to eat. Anticipating their offer of *chicha,* I hurriedly opened a tin of C-rations and made them an offer, but they refused – which was also customary. My intestines were grumbling, so I made a quick dash into the jungle to relieve myself. The Indians knew full well why I darted into the trees, and looked at each other questioningly. They couldn't understand why I would defile the jungle like that when the river was so readily available.

I watched the three pull out their rifles from the pile of gear at the center of the canoe. These were old, rusted, and seldom used rifles of twenty-two caliber. The leader proudly displayed the shells I had given him in trade for the ride, and all three men quickly but quietly eased into the thick jungle. Being without gun, I remained by the boat.

Within minutes I began hearing the popping of the twenty-twos. Half an hour later, they emerged from the trees, but not alone. With them were four bleeding and dying iguanas; the streaking red contrasted brilliantly against their bright green skin color. Each as long as a man's arm; two were shot in the head, one on the side, and one in the chest.

I had never seen an iguana before, which tempted me to finger one on their leathery skin. As I did, the nearly dead animal wiggled its tough jagged spine in defiance and tried to show its full mouth of sharp uneven teeth.

It sure was one ugly animal!

Without doubt, these animals must be a stunted descendant of the dinosaurs. For the Cuna their meat is considered a delicacy any time.

With the assurance of iguana meat for dinner and the anticipation of reaching home by nightfall, the lighthearted men again set the canoe in motion up the Rio Ipeti.

I was not as happy. In a foolish attempt to keep my boots dry, I wore them only sparingly since leaving Maje. My feet had become red, bruised, and wrinkled from pushing the boat off the rocky river bottom. And naturally, the further up the Ipeti we went the more often was it necessary to jump into the river and push. Plus, the pant-legs of my Levis' were rolled to my knees and were continually wet, causing a nasty irritation in my crotch area. My muscles were sore from sleeping on the ground and pushing and pulling the canoe.

Worst of all, my unsettled stomach kept me in a state of anxiety – never knowing when I would require the leader to find a spot for me to get out of the boat and relieve myself. They were, however, satisfied with my new skill of doing it in the river. It was a lot easier to clean myself. And, I was running out of toilet paper in the C-Ration boxes.

By the time our *piraqua* reached the village of Ipeti, I was, to say the least, feeling miserable.

*   *   *   *   *

Dusk had comfortably settled on the jungle when we finally rested the canoe on the riverbank at Ipeti. There to meet the returning travelers were men, women and children of all ages. In fact, the whole village showed up – about fifteen in all.

Beneath the usual cheerful greetings associated with homecomings, I sensed a feeling of collective despair; although at the time I had learned only two Cuna words:

- *yes* "eye"
- *no* "satte";

and was working on a third:

- *eat* "kunne".

Most of the villagers glanced at me with a curious indifference, and continued their rapid-fire conversation. The faces of my fellow travelers became emotionally flat as they nodded their heads in solemn understanding. Hurriedly, they unloaded the needed supplies from the *piraqua* by a train of shadowy figures rushing to and from the village huts in the closing moments of daylight; a village nearly identical to Maje but without the missionary.

I was standing alone on the soft earthen riverbank in the near darkness when a young boy about ten or eleven years old came to my rescue. He picked up my saddle-bags and led the way to an empty *congresso* (meeting hall). On the way to the large hut a group of younger children followed. This *congresso*, one of two in the village, was empty and dark until the same boy lit a small wick protruding from a container of kerosene. I stood by the illuminating flame, shivering in the chilly night air and wondering what to do next. The children stared, and occasionally giggled.

My stampeding thoughts were soon corralled when two men entered the building and came into the circle of light. The younger of the two introduced himself, in very good English, as *Maurice* and introduced the elder Cuna beside him as "my Chief". I was completely flabbergasted! Who would ever have thought that deep in the Darien Jungle a Cuna speaking near perfect English would be found? Maurice quickly explained himself by saying he had worked many months in the Panama Canal Zone where he learned to speak English. It was a great pleasure for him to speak in English, he said, because he had few opportunities to do so in the jungle. He shared a few personal facts about himself, and I explained my purpose of being in the Darien and at Ipeti. The Chief remained silent; as our three dark shadows shown unevenly silhouetted on the bamboo wall, as if in Plato's Allegory of the Cave.

Maurice went on to explain why the villagers were disturbed: The day before our arrival, a five year old child had wandered near a large kettle of boiling liquid and somehow managed to tip it over, spilling the scalding contents on his naked body. Without rapid medical assistance or quick transportation to a medical facility there was little hope for the child. Chepo, the closest facility was at least two and a half days away. The villagers were reluctant to use modern medical facilities; relying instead on the local shaman.

Maurice asked if I had any medicine. I quickly jerked open the saddle-bags and grabbed the small first-aid kit, and followed the two men into the other large hut. This *congresso* was jammed with people, and nearly everyone had a kerosene lantern or candle.

They were crowded around a single small hammock. A few whispers quickly passed through the onlookers when they noticed a foreigner in their mist. Nearing the hammock, I saw the mother of the child almost force-feeding the baby boy a small piece of fish and the recently received rice. I quietly asked Maurice to persuade the mother that feeding the child could do more harm than good at this stage for the burnt child. On the other side of the child was a weathered old man placing various large leaves on the boy; a shaman, I presumed. He gave me a hard look as if I were intruding. Maurice and the shaman exchanged a few words. Not allowing me to touch the boy's body, the shaman raised the leaves for us to observe the scalded damage.

The sight was nausea inducing. Over fifty per cent of the front of his body was covered with first and second degree burns; the worst of which were on his stomach and thighs; even his genitals. The more intensely scalded areas looked like red, raw meat infected with a white fungus and scraped with a dull knife. His skin looked horrible; some blistered, some without form. Some of the white and wrinkled skin barely clung to the muscle.

The child remained eerily calm as if nothing had happened – probably in some stage of shock. Only the infrequent blinking of his eyelids over his round black eyes changed his lack of expression. Within minutes he began to vomit the undigested fish and rice he had been fed minutes before; discharging the spew down his chin and left arm onto a portion of the scalded area. The mother rushed to wipe away the undigested food with a multi-colored dirty rag. She looked at the shaman and glanced at me pleading for help.

I had no formal medical training and had forgotten whatever treatments I may have learned during survival training in the military. But instinctively I knew I had to do everything within my power to help the child.

I began talking with Maurice, telling him I needed some clean cold water, hot water and white cloths. This initiated a struggle between Maurice and the shaman – which Maurice won, because the shaman was not a *real* shaman, only an elder of the clan acting as a shaman.

As Maurice issued the orders for water and rags, the congresso broke into quiet talking and disordered movement. The cold water came quickly; and then the hot. But to our dismay there was no white cloth available in the entire village.

I had a very small first-aide kit in my saddle bags and a white handkerchief in my back pocket. As I rinsed the handkerchief in the hot, another struggle ensued because the mother didn't want me touching the child. The mother won.

I talked Maurice through what I would have done. He wiped off the remaining undigested food and other areas that looked dirty or pussy with the warmed handkerchief. Some of the child's skin pulled away. The handkerchief was then rinsed in the cold water and laid over the largest scalded area. The procedure was repeated every five or ten minutes.

In my kit were a small can of suntan paste, and a short length of gauze.

I didn't know if the suntan paste would help, but I instructed Maurice to wipe it on around the edges of the worst scalded areas. Cutting the gauze into short strips with my knife, Maurice placed the strips over the child's chest and upper legs. A villager came close and placed a palm leaf from a banana tree over his body.

The only thing left was to encourage the mother to give him plenty of water to drink, and, if possible, to not move him.

After that, my resources were exhausted and I was physically and mentally spent. It had been a very long day.

*   *   *   *   *

Slowly I backed away from the circling crowd who, by this time, had once again fixed their attention on the mother and child, to carry my equipment to a secluded corner at the far end of the hut. Feeling a rumble in my stomach and being certain no eyes were on me, I dropped the bags and ran outside into the unfamiliar night for a projectile defecation.

The intestinal wastage had become water-thin by this time, and soon I would be unable to control my bowel movements for any length of time; not knowing if it was dysentery or diarrhea. I only knew there was sweat on my forehead, my hands were shaking, and my energy was depleted. I wanted to curl up on the dark ground anywhere and try to sleep forever.

Unsteady and disoriented, I stumbled my way back to the congresso and tied my hammock between two support rafters of the hut. I just sat there, ankles crossed, blankly staring at these human beings who carve a life out of the complexity of the jungle. What were they *really* like?

I wonder if they think about the same things? What are their hopes and dreams? What preoccupies most of their

thoughts just before sleep, after the day has been survived? Do they ponder where shooting stars come from, and if there is life on other planets? They eat, drink, sleep, and have sex; laugh and cry and are tight with each other. But they don't seem restless like me. Who was I tight with? I wonder if they are also searching for some truth. Do they believe in God? Is there a bunch of mini-Gods, or just God and us? What the hell am I doing here, anyway?
__Damn Kerouac!__

Maurice separated himself from the group and sat beside me. I conveyed my sorrow and desire to do more, but we silently understood there was little more – if anything – that could be done to save the scalded child. It was best to continue my journey and in the morning he would show me the path leading to the Chucunaque River. He spoke about a truck and a road, but I had no idea what he was talking about; and didn't have the energy to pursue it.

After Maurice returned to the crowd surrounding the child, I thought about the helpless child and didn't care who lived or died. At that moment I didn't care about anybody or anything – only my own depressing miseries. I was wet, cold, hungry, exhausted, and with fever. My feet were tender and sore. I had severe stomach cramps and the insect bites still bothered me. My mind was so preoccupied with pain I begged it to stop. I prayed for sleep, even though I knew it would be interrupted by the spastic calls of my bowels. For a long while everything was completely blurred. The building swirled around and around. Then there was nothingness.

Somehow I endured a little sleep.

*   *   *   *   *

Dawn came with a somber ashen silence. The grayness slowly crept its way into the congresso through the bamboo slits and across the earthen floor displaying an empty hall. It was all so dreamlike, so surreal. The small hammock, where only a few hours ago the injured boy had lain, was now empty; no people, no fire. Nothing!

The far corners of the hut were like dark caverns. Only the stout poles holding the thatched roof seemed ready to accept the weight of the new day as more light pushed through the doorway. Even after Maurice brought me a breakfast and departed without a word, I continued to feel outside of myself, outside of the mainstream of thought – outside reality.

No sign of Cuna life or the events of the past night existed. Desperately I tried recalling the events of the previous evening: the treatment of the boy, the talks with Maurice, collapsing in my hammock, and at least 3 times during the night being forced outside with runny stools. But during the entire night, from what I remembered, the tribesmen maintained vigilance and a fire beside the child. Now they were gone.

Still weak and confused, I rolled my sleeping gear and waited for Maurice. During the wait, I made two more quick trips to the river-banks to let the wastage run out. But I was feeling a little stronger after the breakfast of rice and a sliver of iguana meat. Soon Maurice came and led me to his canoe; purposefully avoiding my questioning stares. Once in the canoe, I settled myself and gear on the bow and Maurice pushed the canoe away from the water's edge at Ipeti and began paddling from the stern.

During the five minute ride, we spoke of many things. He admitted to feeling disenchanted with the modern way of life in the Canal Zone and chose to return to the more simple life of his home in the jungle. The air was clean, the water fresh, and plenty of meat and fish to eat. He had the closeness of his tribesmen and plenty of huts in which to live. With only these necessities to occupy his mind he was happy. He knew I was agreeing with him to be polite.

However, with each word, I could feel his dilemma between the natural life in the jungle and complexity of the more "civilized" world. There were payoffs to both ways of living: the primitive lack of medical attention for the scalded child, versus the modern disconnectedness of a fatherless childhood.

I was about to question him further, especially about the child, when the canoe bumped into the soft mud of the river bank. There was a clearing in the trees showing a trailhead. While unloading my equipment, Maurice said, this was the pathway leading to the Chucunaque River. He led me down the first hundred yards of the path; repeating the story about a truck road within several days walking time. I assumed he was referring to a road large enough on which a truck could travel.

Abruptly he stopped and said: "The boy, he dies." Not knowing whether he meant the boy *will* die or he *had* died, I only uttered "Si" in return.

Neither of us wanted to pursue the topic any further so we made our farewells. I gave this kind Cuna Indian the last fishing hook I had along with a short length of cat-gut fishing line. He thanked me, we shook hands and parted with a great feeling of brotherly affection. Heading in opposite directions – different lives, different worlds – I never looked back.

*   *   *   *   *

The path was well used and wide, for jungle conditions. For the first few miles only minor obstructions broke the rhythm of my walking. Though weak and tired, I still marveled at the beauty of the closely-knitted plant life. Swarms of green leaves arched overhead supported by intermingling branches with hanging vines rivaling any botanical gardens. I was in a leafy green tunnel shading the moist black earth from the burning sun, leaving waffled impressions from the bottom of my boots with each step.

The hardships of the past days were nearly forgotten, suppressed by the aura of the enchanted jungle – no dusty soda bottles, no cigarette wrappings, and no rusting tin-cans. There was only my persistent self and the glory of nature. I rarely looked back, and stopped only for necessities.

I didn't have the slightest notion where I was going or what was before me. And this began to raise my spirits. All I knew, or cared about was that my general direction was easterly.

"Oops! There goes a snake slivering across my path." It was brownish and olive colored with dark triangles on its scales, about four or five feet long. It was thin and didn't want to bother me, quickly heading off into the brush to my right. Except for its length, I was unafraid.

*A little reality check! My research proved the snake to be a **fer-de-lance**. Without doubt, one of the more deadly snakes in the world.*

I was feeling a bit stronger now. The past few days of idleness and despair were soon forgotten. The saddle-bags rested on my shoulders swaying left to right with each step. The rolled sleeping gear tied with rope which slung over my shoulder also swayed. My right hand firmly gripped the machete. I felt as if I could have gone on in this way forever.

I wanted to cover as much ground as possible before the jungle shrubbery swallowed the trail, as I knew it would. Also, I had hopes of sweating the feverish dysentery out of my body; it seemed to be subsiding, but still required intermittent stops.

The combination of walking, the heat, and humidity opened up every pore in my skin. I began to sweat, slowly at first. Then, as if nature opened a spigot, perspiration gushed from my skin, drenching my entire body. This loosened my muscles, allowing my pace to quicken. My protective jacket stuck tenaciously to my wet back, and even the heavy dungarees showed uneven patches of sweat stains. Streams of sweat ran down my forehead and onto my cheeks allowing me to taste the salt.

Still I continued onward, stopping now and then for a sip of water from the canteen.

Like involuntary muscles, my legs kept moving ahead; one foot up and the other one down; one foot up and one foot down; one foot up... Unemotional and without commands from my brain; up, down; up, down.

The saddle-bags, resting on my chest, felt like a hammer pounding at my lungs lessening my breathing capacity. Both straps chafed at my shoulder muscles and the rope wrapped around the sleeping gear gnawed constantly at my right collar bone. Switching, it then gnawed at my left collar bone.

Each new mound or hill of the uneven jungle terrain contained a host of obstructions or was home to its own family of insects ready to feed off me, breaking my stride. Everything wanted to stop my forward progress.

On rare occasions the sunlight found a way between the overhanging foliage allowing me to feel its healing rays. But I soon learned to despise the shanks of brightness breaking through the green canopy, because it meant a fallen tree was lying across my path, usually with a thick tree trunk and broken branches piled high. Some I could hop over and some I could climb over, but most times I was forced to hack my way around. Every detour meant the ever present possibility of losing the original trail after completing the semi-circle.

Many times I was unable to find the trail and found myself lost in the dense bushes where upright walking was impossible. I was forced to push my way through the overgrowth with my back bent like an old man or an ancient primate; sometimes I had to crawl on my knees. Lost and directionless for hours, I was in a constant struggle against the unforgiving vegetation.

Somehow though, I always managed to maintain contact with what I thought was the main path.

*   *   *   *   *

Eventually the jungle began to absorb the sun. My body had endured enough pain and misery. Head pounding, feet sore, and skin sodden with sweat, I decided to make camp and call it a day.

Haphazardly, I cleared a small area of jungle floor next to the trail, strung the hammock between two trees, and stretched the mosquito net over the top. With a great effort I slowly bent over and unbuckled my boots. And, after sliding off the sweaty military socks, I took a long look at my achy feet. On the little toe of each foot was a great blister, shining like melted candle wax and pulsating with each heart beat. I fingered them gently, then massaged the remaining toes and the rest of my feet.

Ever so slowly I lifted my legs into the hammock one at a time and stretched my throbbing muscles full length on the canvas with a sigh of relief. For the first time since entering the Darien Jungle my throat called for more water. My stomach craved more of the rice and iguana meat I had eaten for breakfast; I had eaten nothing since. But I neither ate nor drank.

Through the misery my mind was able to find two bright spots for the day: one was in knowing I had covered about twenty air-miles since leaving Ipeti, later calculated to be only ten miles; and two was the comfort in feeling the intestinal disorder had somehow resolved itself; it was no longer bothering me.

I just lay there with my hands folded over my chest watching the last grey speck of light turning into total blackness; I was too tired to remove the damp clothing from my body.

And sleep would not come.

The night in the hammock was spent tossing and turning, with sudden interruptions caused by "attacks" of the itching bug bites on the lower parts of my legs and the accompanying electric shocks.

Then the scratching began!

I started by raising my trouser cuffs knee high and lightly scratched with my fingernails. When the calves became too tender, I rubbed the bites with my fingers and palms hoping the friction would satisfy the maddening urge. And it did satisfy – for about five minutes. And again, the scratching would begin. I was unable to discipline myself to *not* scratch.

Obsessed with this modicum of satisfaction, I scratched up the right leg to the knee, behind the knee, and all the way to below the ankle. I would then switch to the left leg and go through the same procedure exactly the same. The clammy feeling of my finger tips told me the scratching had led to bleeding. But it didn't stop me from more scratching. In a strange way, the scratching was so satisfying. Sometimes I would lower my trouser cuffs hoping this would reduce the urge. But it didn't.

Like a jumping toothache the incessant itching returned and, unable to control the impulse, I thrust my long nails into the madness. Sometimes both hands were scratching. I tried spitting on my finger tips and rubbed the saliva onto the open bites hoping the liquid would cure the eternal itching. But it didn't!

It felt as if every nerve ending in my body was on fire, burning with excitement. Illusions of hundreds of tiny insects crawling over every inch of my skin, through my hair, and into my body cavity filled my thoughts. I wanted to run so far and fast that the leeches would lose their grip on my skin; I wanted to run away into the void, nowhere into the black void.

But there was nowhere to go, nobody to help, nothing to do but persevere.

Exhaustion eventually overcame my tortured mind and body. And, like any fire left without stoking, the itching died out. I slept perhaps an hour in the cooling cinders of the early daylight. With a sigh of relief at the sight of the dull trees surrounding me, I became once again occupied with the problems of surviving for another day.

*   *   *   *   *

The entry in my diary notes for February 28, 1965:

Arose. Well, I'm still alive! Body feels stiff as a board. Stripped naked and scraped ticks off my body – about sixty in all, I'm guessing. Legs red and sore from too much scratching last night. Blisters still very tender. Not much water left, very thirsty and hungry – mostly thirsty. Decided to eat a can of pork and beans for breakfast, then continued down the trail. Found some stagnant water in a dry creek bed but refused to drink, too dirty even for the Halazone tablets. Trail gradually narrowed to almost nothing. Had to use the machete almost constantly. So thirsty – only a few ounces left. Rustling of the tree leaves sound like running water – every sound, everything reminds me of water. Only hope is to find the Canazas or Chucunaque tomorrow. Many dried creek beds but no water. Got lost (several times) and stayed lost for hours. But do believe in those compasses, man! And I'd already be dead without a machete. Growing weak and tired. Walking very slowly now. Didn't take a shit today and don't know if that is good or bad. Made camp by a dried creek bed. Thinking about an icy root beer float, milk shakes, a cold beer – anything liquid. Cleared off the blood-sucking ticks again. Even now, sitting on the hammock and writing this in the dim light, I somehow feel secretly good to know soon I'll be satisfying that urge to scratch the bites. Can't help it – the only joy I know now. Easy to understand masochism. Hope for water tomorrow, with luck maybe a river. I long for the sound of a human voice, to see another person, to listen to music, the sight of the ocean. That's it for today. Must try to keep notes safe and in good order.

*   *   *   *   *

The first day of March I arose and repeated the mantra: "Well, I'm still alive." I said this aloud to myself every morning to reassure myself that I *was*, in fact, alive. I undressed and began, what was to become, the daily habit of inspecting myself for ticks and other leeching insects. I was happy to find that only a few blood-suckers had burrowed their heads into my skin during the night. Again, most were concentrated around the old bites on my calves and ankles.

Feeling "cleansed" for the moment, I dressed and continued down the trail.

Thoughts of thirst, hunger, and my position on the map (in that order) agitated my mind.

All the water was gone!

I raised the canteen to my lips and tilted my head back. A few drops of water fell onto my tongue, but I could hardly swallow. I licked the inside of the canteen cap to moisten my tongue. It didn't help much. And now the hunger pains were becoming even stronger! I was foolish enough to eat a few cans of the C-rations while staying at the mission in Maje, hoping to relieve their burden. I left Maje with only five cans remaining in the saddle bags. One can was eaten on the trip upriver to Ipeti, and one yesterday. That left me with three cans. Being uncertain of the future, I would have to stave off the hunger pains as long as possible. There was probably enough life-sustaining energy in the three cans of nutrition for almost a week – or at least, that was my thinking. By that time, I felt certain I would be at or near El Real – the main community of the Darien.

I could only guess my position on the map. For the past two days I had been traveling east by south; walking between the Rio Canazas and a low mountain range in what appeared to be approximately five air-miles on the map. WRONG! I also estimated the distance between Ipeti and the Canazas was about fifteen air-miles. WRONG, AGAIN!

How could I accurately calculate my position?

Because I was not very good at math, I often tell this funny story of when I was in a 10th grade high school math class in Columbia, PA. Everyone was taking a math test and the teacher – a big burly football coach – walked around the classroom observing. As he looked over my shoulder he let out a big belly laugh. And, of course, I was embarrassed. He then shared with the rest of the class: "Now here in Chet. He writes the problem down, does the calculations wrong, but gets the correct answer." And everyone laughed.

The compass was good, but the map was terrible. I should have reached that river by this time. I could have missed the junction of the rivers. On the map, it appeared as if the

Chucunaque was only thirty air-miles due east from Ipeti. And, calculating ten miles a day, it was a three-day walk. But I could only estimate, really guess how far I'd walked.

No good to keep guessing here. I just have to keep moving. I know I'm going in the right direction.

Groaning as my back bent forward to pick up all the gear, I started walking. The tempo was slow at first owing to my stiff muscles and joints. But after fifteen or twenty minutes I loosened up and was taking normal strides.

No sooner had my body become flexible when the trail suddenly disappeared and I was again lost. Stumbling through the sticky bush, I saw what appeared to be *the* path, clear-cut and heading easterly. I followed it, unaware of the shock I was about to see.

Fifty yards later, I walked straight to the most gigantic anthill I had ever seen - or imagined. It stood at least a foot to two higher than my five foot eight inch frame, and looked like a great pile of pulverized sawdust – only with thousands of large dark ants streaming in and out of a dozen holes; especially at the top. So perfectly formed was this high yellowish mound it looked almost man-made. It was surrounded by several smaller, disfigured, and uninhabited anthills, and looked like a miniature landscape of the foothills to a mountain; in severe contrast to the surrounding and overhanging jungle.

Fifteen seconds was all the time I spent at the anthill. It took fifteen seconds for me to gaze at the wonder of it all, and then to realize the danger!

It wasn't long before hundreds of these large red ants were streaming over my boots and up my pant legs; some had already found their way under my clothing and were biting with their sharp prickly claws. How did they get to me so quickly? Automatically, I began stomping my feet to the ground hoping to knock them off. Then I slapped my trousers and boots, panicked by their overwhelming numbers. In a terror-stricken instant with thoughts of being eaten alive, I dashed into the woods, arms flailing and equipment flopping.

They were "sail ants", or leaf-cutters. I had seen plenty of them along the path before, but never in these numbers. They would march along a tiny path of fresh earth barren of vegetation holding their freshly cut piece of leaf in an upright position resembling a green sail.

They marched almost in cadence, like something out of "Fantasia". Never had I seen a path cut out of the jungle floor this wide. Never had the jungle seemed more intimidating, more unforgiving.

*   *   *   *   *

As time wore on, my forward motion slowed. The jungle was coming alive! It had a life of its own; a gigantic organism pulsating with heat, flashing lights, vibrating sounds, unending smells, changing colors... I wanted to be part of it. My eyes became focused and keen to every movement, then unfocused like gazing at a giant Monet. My skin was ultra-sensitive to the vegetation, absorbing its life-giving moisture directly into my blood. The lore of water was all around. The soft breeze carried by a nymph whispered between the uneven trees with the beckoning sounds of rippling water. A pair of exotic birds darted past, flashing their bright green and yellow feathers. I wanted to be transformed, to be transparent and float through the jungle like a Goddess of Nature.

Is this it? Is this it? Is this what I came for? Is this what I'm looking for? It this what it's all about? Nobody here! Nobody to share this with. The loneliness feels heavy. Is this what Kerouac experienced? The beatific vision?

But I was stuck in reality. The reality was my thirst, and the possibility of dying of dehydration. And the reality was, free from all social distractions and running out of ways to deny, I was beginning to sense a great tension; a relentless, omnipresent, surrounding *tension*. I wasn't sure what it was or where it came from. It just seemed to naturally exist between me and the jungle; man and nature; things and values. How am I to relieve this tension?

*   *   *   *   *

My thirst for water had, by this time, grown to obsession. The inside of my mouth was like dead skin, and my throat felt like an empty sand bag. My survival instincts took all reasoning!

I need water! And I need it _now_! I will do _anything_ for water – _anything_! Where can I find water? There _must_ be water here _someplace_!

I dropped all equipment, except the machete, and began randomly cutting all the thick fibrous plants around me to suck their ends for moisture. But I coughed, choked, and spit out the white foamy substance. I tried pulling plants from the ground hoping to see water beneath the roots. I dug directly into the darkened earth hoping to strike a rich water source. Nothing! I only succeeded in temporarily losing the spot where the equipment was.

Exhausted, I fell to the ground and raised my back against a decayed log.

I closed my eyes and searched the deepest recess of my mind, hoping for a memory, an idea, anything that would help me get the life-sustaining water.

Going through my years of military training, I remembered what one of my sergeants said and constantly repeated: "A soldier should never die of thirst in the jungle. A soldier should never die of thirst in the jungle."

But why? Why? Why? Why should a soldier never die of
thirst in the jungle? Was it in the trees, the plants, the vines...?
That's it! THE VINES!

It was in the vines. I jumped to my feet and ran into the
brush stopping by a large tree with dozens of hanging vines.
Now, was it the top of the vine or the bottom to cut first? I didn't
care! I stretched my arm as high and began hacking at the closest
brown vine of three inch diameter with the machete. With the top
severed, I sliced off the bottom with two quick whacks of the
machete leaving me with a seven foot length of juicy vine. With
outstretched arms I raised the piece of vine into the air and rested
the top against a low branch.

Raising the neatly cut bottom of the vine near my mouth,
I peered down at the soft clean wood – but saw nothing.

Then, like sparkling beads of early morning dew,
moisture appeared. Slowly the beads grew into large drops of
clear water, and I licked them off. Eventually, a small amount of
the life-sustaining liquid trickled in my mouth. It was delicious!
Then, more water came. My outstretched arms were burning for
relief, but I wanted the fresh water to continue until I had a full
swallow of water; and I did.

For some unknown reason the dripping stopped!

Again I harkened to my survival training. Lowering the
vine, I cut about fifteen inches off the top and again raised the
bottom to my lips. Again the trickle of water appeared and began
running into my mouth; and continued this process until only a
stub of the vine remained. But with each cutting, less and less
water came through its narrow fleshy fibers. I had gained at least
a mouthful of water, and was momentarily satisfied.

A sudden shock ran through me! Having been disoriented
by the thirst, I didn't know where the saddle-bags and sleeping
gear had been dropped. For a frenzied hour I was in a state of
panic without the equipment. By placing my shirt on the tree of
the cut vines, I moved in an enlarging spiral circle further and

further away until the equipment was found conspicuously lying where it had been dropped.

Confidence rising with the new-found skill of obtaining water, I began devising a method for capturing larger quantities. I grabbed an empty C-ration can from the saddle bags and placed it on a cleared spot on the ground. Next I chopped off six or seven more vines of an even greater diameter (four or five inches) and rested them on a nearby log with their bottoms aimed into the can. The dripping began and eventually I gained four or five ounces. Slowly I drank it; relishing each swallow as it went across my tongue and down my throat. It had a brackish taste and was littered with small pieces of bark – but life sustaining. Water never tasted so good!

Again, determination exceeded my skills.

I've thought a lot about water ever since. What fascinates me most about water is the illogic of it all. Water is composed of two highly flammable chemicals – hydrogen and oxygen. Who could have predicted that when combined – two hydrogen and one oxygen – liquid water would be produced and used to douse fire? Totally illogical.

*And this leads to thoughts about **causes**. What caused this, and what caused that? What caused the earth and the universe? The Big Bang doesn't satisfy me. If this were so, there had to have been **something** there to be exploded. Where did **that** come from? Is there a First Cause? And is the First Cause and Uncaused cause? A First Thought? A First Person?*

I continued this process of draining water from the vines until the canteen was once again full. With my thirst and the need for water satisfied, I stumbled around until I found the trail. Full of confidence but emptied of energy my forward progress continued in the usual southeasterly direction.

*   *   *   *   *

Hunger now saturated my mind and dominated my tortured body. Slowly over the past two weeks my muscles had become sapped of their strength. I had not eaten for over thirty hours (the rice and iguana meat), and only one can of C-rations since leaving Ipeti three days before. It wasn't just the walking that tired me, but the *fight* against the un-groomed jungle for each step of the way; slashing the bushes blocking the trail, climbing over and under logs, and struggling uphill and resisting gravity on the downhill slide.

I wouldn't spit for fear of losing a single morsel of food that could be wedged somewhere between my teeth or hidden in the recesses of my mouth. I gargled each sip of water before swallowing One calorie of energy may be all I needed to carry me over the next obstacle, over the next hill to the river – to food. Briefly, I saw several howler monkeys jumping through the trees, and listened to their shrill cries mocking my thought of seeing them skinned and roasted on a silver platter served on a white tablecloth. The small plant growth reminded me of a sweet tossed salad. The insects gave the appearance of aromatic spices.

If I only had a gun!

But I refused to stop my forward movement. As long as I had energy to walk, I vowed to continue.

In time, I began to notice an increasing number of fallen trees; large trees perhaps three or four feet in diameter. They showed no signs of decay. Upon a closer examination, it was obvious each one had been *sawed* off near the base of the trunk – not fallen naturally. Also, they appeared to have been cut within the past several weeks – a month at the most. This gave my dwindling confidence a boost, and prompted a definite feeling that *something* was near.

At this point, rising spirits could not overcome a depleted body. The body and mind were disconnected, as two separate entities. My brain/mind forced deliberate orders commanding my legs and arms to move: now step, now chop, now breathe, now climb; now step, now chop now breath... No muscles seemed involuntary, nothing was easy. The hostile environment all around was beyond control; mutinous, rebellious.

Hmm, just like me. But I'm too hungry to think about it.

The light brush of my arm against a tree limb or the weeds catching and momentarily holding my boots fought to deter my forward motion. Obstructing branches had to be cut, sharp thorny weeds jabbed through my clothing and into my skin, and the always unruly terrain made walking, unobstructed walking, impossible.

The never ending battle against the insurgent jungle continued as I approached the base of an unusually steep hill. Peering up, I doubted if I could reach the top. But I had to try; had to see if salvation was at the top.

Slowly I began the ascent, preserving energy by barely raising each boot only a minimum off the ground while restricting each body movement to the bare necessities; sometimes using my arms to lift my legs. Occasionally, I was compelled to pause on both knees and catch my breath. This hill was no higher than others behind me, but in my weakened condition the top of this one looked unattainable. But some unrevealed energy reserve kept me going.

A few yards from the top, an exposed root showed itself protruding from the ground like a wooden stirrup. The sight of this root registered mentally; my brain issued an order to lift the left foot over it; but my leg refused to obey.

My left boot became momentarily stuck in the well-anchored root.

Tripping, I stumbled forward in a vain attempt to avoid falling. But I fell with a grunt and landed face-first in the dirt as I neared the hilltop.

I just laid there for a while, too exhausted to get up. Salty sweat streamed down my forehead burning my eyes and blurring my vision. I could barely lift my head or move my hands. I peered at the ground only inches away, trying to focus and make the dizzy spots go away. My onrushing breath scattered flaky specks of dust and tiny pieces of bark onto my hands spread before me. I felt pieces of dirt going deeper and deeper down my moist throat with each gasp.

A community of ants, ticks and sundry insects scurried around in chaos, under and over the obstacles in their environment in search of each other. I almost snickered at the comparison. Were we just like them or were they just like us? At that moment I felt as if I were fodder for the jungle; food for its evolutionary growth. I was about to become one with the jungle.

Is this it? What a way to go! Alone; in a jungle nobody ever heard of; too young; unfulfilled; never had a family of my own. It sure would be nice to see my mother again; my sister and brother too. I sure gave them a lot of heartache. I'd screwed a lot of women, but never had a <u>real</u> relationship. I guess I'll never hear the truth to the whispers I fathered a child; maybe more.

My death would not make the headlines in any newspaper even if anyone were unfortunate enough to find my body before it was fully consumed by the living earth. And, except for relatives and a few friends, I would be forgotten. It would be just another death in the forbidden jungle; just another lost soul into the unknown.

Tears welled in my eyes and I began to weep. I was despondent and believed I was about to die. My body seemed unable to carry me. It would have been so easy to just die there, to give up.

Ha, some shakedown cruise!

I then began to think about life after death; as I had done many times. I had no way of being certain about it – nor did anyone else. Always there was fear connected with these thoughts. It was the *uncertainty* of it all. I had no experiences to validate anything one way or the other. Always the conversations with myself would lead to imagining a void, a nothingness.

> ***I'm not going to just <u>let</u> myself die. If I die, I die. But it's not going to happen for the lack of trying. My mind is stronger than that. I can <u>will</u> my self into motion, no matter how slowly. The jungle is going to have to kill me; I'm not going to kill myself.***

The innate fear and the crawling insects over my body shocked me into reality. A biting red ant found its way to the hairs in my left nostril. With a surprising amount of agility I raised to my knees and picked the ant out of my nose, then brushed the remaining bugs, bark, and dirt from my clothing.

Doing so, my eyes naturally looked downward from the top of the hill.

I doubted what I saw!

Not more than a hundred yards ahead was a *dirt road* shining in the evening sunlight like a golden river! My mind must be playing tricks with me; hallucinating. I could not have been more surprised if it had been a dragon, an elephant, or Jesus Christ himself.

I stumbled toward it, terrified it was only a figment of my imagination. Once there, I stomped the clay dirt of the road twice with my boots making absolutely certain it was real. Not only was it real, but it also showed signs of recent use; possibly the tire tracks of a large vehicle. The compass reading showed the road was heading in a north-south direction. I was lucky enough to have found the road even though it wasn't going in my east-west way.

After a few moments I was overcome by disillusionment.

Had I managed to travel in a circle? Was I back in the Jenene area near where this jungle odyssey began? I didn't care! The road had to lead *somewhere*. To where, I didn't care. Walking north, I knew my chances of getting to a river would be faster than a southerly route. And, compared to the jungle trails, walking the dirt road was nearly effortless; no tugging branches, no sharp thorns, no thick brush, no soggy ditches, and no sharp ridges. There was only the soft beautiful dust of this wide road sprinkling the top of my boots as I ambled slowly around the first bend.

After walking for only a few hundred yards, a second extraordinary sight came into view: a juicy-looking *orange* appeared lying in the middle of the road. Like a jeweler handling a precious stone, I picked the fruit up, turned it slowly around, and gently squeezed it several times. Looking for the exact angle to cut, I open it into four equal sections; amazed at the lack of aging or bruising. To not lose one drop of liquid, I licked the juice from my knife and sucked the surface nectar from each of the slices.

Unable to hold back, I proceeded to eat every bit of the orange; the flesh, skin, seeds, inner stem, and all. Even the normally bitter taste of the peelings suddenly tasted incredibly delicious. I could actually feel the nutrition in the orange transforming, bursting into energy for my body. Charging through the jungle gauntlet from sun-up to sun-down for two weeks had thwarted my stomach past its sensitivity for solid foods.

From within, I could actually feel the sensation of the food bursting into energy. It was as if a million tiny explosions ignited at once conquering the fatigue – even death. The microscopic bursts radiated throughout my body, from the top of my head to the bottom of my toes. Finally, I once again felt like moving.

It was amazing how one small orange fruit made me feel so alive.

Sitting on the edge of the treasured road, I allowed for the full transformation of the orange from near-extinction to life preservation; watching the sun sink deeper into the wooded forest. For the moment, I was content.

The time of contentment was short-lived – as always - when suddenly I heard the undeniable sound of a loud combustion engine. Gradually the sound of the piston popping machine became louder and louder until I was certain it was coming toward me.

Then, spewing clouds of dust from both sides, a *truck* came charging down the road! Surprise was overcome by happiness and joy!

Surely, I must be one of the luckiest guys in the world? First the road, then the orange, now a truck! Come to think of it, I was <u>born</u> lucky! According to family folklore a black man kissed me shortly after birth – a sure sign of good luck. His name was Buck so this became my nickname. (Buck was the first veteran of World War II returning to our hometown as a prisoner of war, and was not recognized. Several months later the son of a prominent (white) attorney returned home under similar conditions and was honored with a parade.)

I bounced up and leaped to the middle of the road waving my arms wildly overhead. Majestically the truck came to a halt in front of me. The cabin was rusted and seemed held together by bailing wire and beads of spot welding. There were no doors or windows, and I could see the floor boards somehow nailed down. It reminded me of an old Army deuce-and-a-half without the canvas top. But for me, it was a beautiful work of art.

In the cabin sat two black skinned Panamanians looking slightly stunned, wondering at the sight of me. The driver asked me in rapid-fire Spanish who I was, where I was coming from, and where I was going. In my tormenting Spanish, I responded that I came from Panama City and was trying to walk to Colombia via the Darien. Adding, I was an American. At this, the driver closed his eyes, shook his head in disbelief, and let out a long loud hissing sound between his teeth.

But thinking they were disinterested and that I was lying or crazy, I desperately blurted out several times: *"Mucho tiempo no aqua, muy hambre. Mucho tiempo no aqua, muy hambre."* Which, when roughly translated, was supposed to mean something like: "It's been a long time since I had water, and I'm very hungry." The driver and his passenger pointed in the direction the truck was heading and said something about a fishing village. I couldn't understand much of what they were trying to say.

I made a quick mental picture of the map and realized the only fishing village for many miles up and down the entire coast of western Panama was Santa Fe; and it was many miles out of my way up the Pacific Coast. The toothless passenger (a sure sign he had spent a lot of time in the sugar cane fields as a youth) pointed in the opposite direction and said something that I again could not comprehend. They seemed reluctant to carry me with them as a passenger.

I thought they were about to leave me standing there, so with great emphasis, I pointed to the bed of the truck and tried to persuade them for permission to climb aboard. The driver too shaking his head no, pointed in the opposite direction. But I was insistent. Finally, and indifferently, he granted permission. I hastily threw my gear on the bed of the truck and climbed on board.

The long bed of the truck had many large pieces of chipped wood, shattered bits of bark, and several heavy semi-rusted chains littering the planked surface. Obviously it was being used to haul timber from one place to another. So, this was what Maurice in Ipeti was telling me! Although I still couldn't understand *how* the truck got there; or even how the smooth dirt road came into being. But it did explain the reason for the many fallen trees I had seen during the earlier part of the day.

The truck sped down the road in a clamber of noise. The vibration of the loose boards under my feet and the bumps in the road would have been uncomfortable under ordinary circumstances. But now it was like riding on the smoothest freeway in the finest most luxurious Rolls Royce, and I didn't care where the truck was going.

As the dust swirled around in the air behind us, I only knew that for the moment at least, I was safe and on my way to *some* safety.

It was pure ecstasy riding through the jungle with the air flowing through my sticky hair with invigorating freshness; postponing a strong desire for sleep. The passing air blew my clothes into a balloon-like bag ventilating my sweaty skin with a chill. My body was numb to any pain, while my mind anticipated the thoughts of human companionship.

It was an unexpected and fit ending to such a difficult day; as the sun ducked from view ushering in the dusk and the darkness of night.

Chapter 5

With only a hint of light remaining, the rattling truck came to a complete stop beside an old dilapidated crane situated near the middle of a freshly cleared circle of jungle growth.

I jumped out of the back and surveyed the area. I was still somewhat uncertain of the motives of the men and of their work. This spot had obviously been chosen to permit easy loading of fallen logs onto the truck which could drive up to the crane, load around the circle, and then go out the same way as coming in.

The truck driver silently led me to the crane and quickly produced a five-gallon bucket of drinking water from under its cabin. I flung myself at the water and began gulping it down from the long-handled pouring cup; stopping between burps to thank him for the kindness. Adding to this, he presented me with four oranges and a package of Panamanian cigarettes.

This helped me understand how I found the orange on the road: they had a plentiful supply of them, and one could have easily fallen from their truck.

Quickly, I began gorging the fruit down my throat, choking on the acidic taste of the juice, when the silence was temporarily interrupted by the entrance of a second truck into the open circle. The truck looked exactly like the other and also contained two Panamanians. When the truck came to a halt, the passenger began barking orders in a loud deep voice. He was obviously the foreman or boss, and soon a generator was humming and the engine of the lifting crane was set in motion.

The driver of the truck that picked me up told the foreman the story of how he found me standing along side the road acting strangely. All four of the loggers huddled together in the shadow of the generator's light talking in low Spanish. The extended shadows of the still bodies reflected on the surrounding trees like an old daguerreotype photograph.

For a while I didn't know if the men were going to accept me as a friend or foe. But soon the foreman broke away from the group and came to me with an offer of pineapple juice and (more) cigarettes; adding a few friendly gestures. Needless to say I hastily swallowed the sweet juice as fast as I could, happy that the men were willing to help me.

Then the four men began the difficult work of loading the nearby scattered logs onto the truck. The crane creaked and groaned, but finally, three giant logs came to rest on the bed of the truck; two on the bottom, one on the top. The foreman motioned for me to climb into the cabin with my equipment and prepare to leave. It was completely dark and, of course, I had no idea where we were going.

With the over-burdening weight of the logs, the roaring engine rebelled and the large tires spun deeper into the soft dirt of the jungle floor. But soon we were moving, and the truck rounded the circle and headed in the direction from which we had come. Then I understood why the driver originally hesitated giving me a ride because he was returning on the same route and would have picked me up on his return trip.

The rugged jungle road, which seemed like a freeway earlier, offered many sharp turns and narrow ditches, adding to the driver's burden of the heavy logs and the loosely held together vehicle. I had no clue where we were going. The driver remained silent as he hustled the truck down the road, lighted by the dull headlights. Never once did he take his eyes off the road in front of him. Like a Grand Prix racer, he performed accurate speed-shifts at the first sign of a slow down as if his life depended on it – and maybe it did.

The tarnished headlights displayed the jungle trees rapidly passing by, only inches away. Once we slowed to a near stop permitting another approaching truck to pass, and the smooth tree leaves of the drooping branches slapped at my right arm. I could see from the illuminated dials of the driver's wrist-watch it was exactly eight o'clock at night. The smooth, shiny, black skin of his face showed faintly from the small light on the dashboard. He was sweating profusely, tired from the stress of driving the heavy load of 3 logs, carrying a foreign passenger, and the dark night.

It was less than an hour when the truck arrived at the main campsite. It looked like a small community of scattered kerosene lanterns, trucks and logging equipment; located next to a river. The driver stopped the truck and told me to go to the largest group of lanterns and pointed in the direction to where dark figures were moving about.

I pulled my equipment off the truck and deliberately moved toward the group of low hung lights and the circle of men around it. The men, all of African descent, were playing poker and using cigarettes for the stakes and were laughing loudly when I appeared before them looking like a fish out of water.

The playing suddenly stopped and, simultaneously, they looked up at me through the dense cigarette smoke. They seemed momentarily shocked, not knowing what to do or say. Finally, one of them – a robust bearded man – stood up and asked me from where I came and to where was I going. Again it was necessary to repeat my unlikely story, ending with my hunger and thirst, but repeating the hunger and thirst part.

For a full ten minutes I stood there trying to string together the words necessary for them to understand my hope of walking into Colombia, South America. Fortunately, my truck driver came to my rescue and told them the story from what he knew – especially the part of how I wolfed down the oranges. I repeated in Spanish of my hunger and thirst.

One of the card players was the camp's cook. He jumped up with a sense of urgency and within a few minutes presented me with a huge tin plate of steaming rice and hot deer meat, followed by a large wooden cup of a grape-flavored drink.

That was the first plate, consumed so fast right before their eyes they must have thought of me as an animal. Quickly the cook gave me a second plate, then a third. After that, I leaned back on one of their chairs and smoked a cigarette, for the moment, completely satisfied. Perhaps I was like a benign virus, adjusting to the body from within.

*   *   *   *   *

The men at the card table displayed a slight uneasiness with me around them. I didn't know if it was a racial thing, their uncertainty about my identity, or what. But soon everybody was relaxed and the men returned to their cards and cigarettes.

With my thirst quenched and my stomach full, I became aware of my filthy body. My skin was sticky and my clothes damp from the constant sweat. Even the breezy truck ride did little to dry me off. Using hand signals and my shaving kit, I communicated the need for a bath. One of the men watching the games, wearing a chic red beret, came forward and led me by flashlight to where they bathed. We followed a lighted a path about fifty yards down the road to a large pile of freshly cut logs jammed in the water by the river's edge. Following him down several partially submerged logs to the running water, I had no way of knowing where I was or which river I was on. I only cared that it was fresh water and I could finally take a bath.

The man in the beret left me with the flashlight, and returned to the poker players.

By the flashlight, I could see I was standing on a large log next to a quiet pool of clean water several feet deep. Undressing, I recklessly jumped in the pool of cool water splashing the water over the upper half of my body. I soaped and scrubbed my body from head to toe; relishing each sensual moment. Afterward, I sat on the long log and let my skin dry in the night air; turning off the flashlight to keep the mosquitoes away.

The lights from the gambling table rippled across the inky-black water as the sound of human voices, reflecting happiness or sorrow, projected into the night air like aliens from a make-believe world.

And even though I desperately needed human contact, I suddenly felt detached from everybody and alone in the universe.

The self-pity lasted only a short time before my aching body reminded me it still needed attention. I switched on the flashlight to inspect my legs. Again, I was dumbfounded by the large number of blood-sucking ticks burrowed in my skin. Again, I began picking them off, one by one. The fingers of my hand moved their bodies back and forth; grown large, round, and dark from my fresh blood. Most were as big as a lentil; depending on how long they had been attached to my skin.

My lower legs were beginning to show the infection and white puss of the previous unhealed bites. When I moved my toes and ankles an aching sensation pulsated in my calves. Added to this was the eternal itching, intensified by the dryness after the soap washing.

I took out the mirror from the shaving-kit for a closer look at my face – which I hadn't seen in over a week. I was shocked! and hardly recognized myself. An unruly red beard covered most of my face and thin lines had formed under my sunken eyes. My once tanned skin was bleached white. Nudging closer to the mirror, I was able to see four or five ticks sticking on the skin of my face; one at the corner of my left eye. I quickly plucked them out.

Next, looking by the lighted mirror, I squatted down for a look at my buttocks with the same shocking results. More ticks! Needless to say, these were removed without delay.

Feeling dirty again, I eased my body back into the water for another bath, hoping the soap would help heal the infections.

Slowly I began to dress but refused to wear what was left of the old stockings. The distasteful part of dressing was putting on the same damp, dirty, smelly clothes – but I had no others.

I returned to the gambling table and met the same man in the red beret. He offered me a seat at the table and a cigarette, and, because of his red beret and black goatee I nicknamed him "Frenchy". Soon everyone at the table was calling him by this name; and we became friends. He made me feel even more accepted by asking the foreman if I could sleep in his hut for the night. Usually there are two men to a hut, so the foreman granted the request because Frenchy's partner was in Santa Fe for a few more days picking up supplies.

By the time the cigarette was finished, I was beginning to feel like one of them. Frenchy disappeared for a while and returned with an already opened bottle of wine, slammed it on the table near us and lifted his thumb above his mouth said something in Spanish which I translated as: "Drink". It was a cheap red wine with a strong smell, a little more than half full, but we savored the sharp taste. Before long the bottle was empty and we were acting a little, if not a lot, tipsy. Deciding it was time, we walked arm-in-arm on a zigzag path with the lantern to his hut.

Once there, and for no reason, I began to laugh; my first good laugh in a very long time. It wasn't just a chuckle, but deep resonating belly laugh lasting until my stomach muscles hardened and hurt. Frenchy chimed in too, and soon we were laughing in concert. Like a two-note song, we landed in our beds one after the other anticipating the sweetness of sleep.

It's been a __long__ time since I drank alcohol. I know it has been a source of problems in my life. In the military, I could drink a fifth of Scotch and still navigate. But, since the trip has started, I haven't craved it.

*   *   *   *   *

It felt so good to be lying in the prone position – the first time since Panama City. I stretched my body from head to toe and fell asleep almost immediately.

Despite the alcohol and the comfort of a prone position, sleep lasted only a few hours. Our hut was only a thatched roof with four corner poles supporting it. Underneath were our two beds made of a low wooden frame with long bamboo slits covered with a thin blanket on which to lay; but with a mosquito net hanging from somewhere above. The sleeplessness and the logging camp atmosphere forced me into past memories.

Now, isn't this ironic! It's been a couple of years since I worked that logging camp in Oregon. What a time that was! Bill Hinkle – still my Dean Moriarty - helped me get the job as a choker-setter. For room and board, his aunt let me stay and work at her motel and bar just outside of Redmond, near Bend. Bill went to Coos Bay as a cutter. I remember the first time I put on my cork boots and walked the length of an 80 foot giant fir; easily 4 feet in diameter. What a thrill! And the first time I actually set the choker and heard the whistle- punk sound the alarm. I watched in total wonder as the cables and pulleys from the spar-trees forced the 3 cinched giants out of the mangled pile of fallen trees, down to the landing close to the yarder-engineer. Even watching them being loaded on the truck for transportation down to the sawmill was cool.

Danger was everywhere! Whole mountain-sides were cleared of standing trees; one fallen on another. Each time we pulled a set of choked trees out of the jammed pile of logs there was always the possibility that this would start an avalanche of trees above us and start them rolling down the mountain. After setting the choker, we had to get the hell out of there as fast as we could, and as far away from the choker as we could. I saw a lot of small avalanches – but nothing major. Cables would break and snap like a whip across the fallen logs. The loose bark often filled the gaps between the spikes in the cork boots to render them slippery and worthless. But the pay was great! That's why we were there; Bill and I were making money for a trip back to Japan and to our boat.

I learned one of my biggest lessons there. The rigging-slinger was this incredible Blackfoot Indian. He was a great boss and could work harder than anyone I ever knew and longer than any person on the crew. He could easily cut a tree down with an axe and make the stump look almost as if it was done with a Stihl. What a guy! Big and handsome. But, to get him on the job was another story. He came to the bar at night and drank like a demon possessed. By comparison, my demon was an infant. He would flirt with any woman, fight any man, and buy drinks until he was broke. Once I had to threaten him with the baseball bat from behind, but he just laughed at me. And, the big question for everyone was: will he make it to work in the morning? The crummy came <u>very</u> early to pick us up; just before dawn.

One morning he caught me catching a little sun on a log while he and the rest of the crew were hard at work. He gave me a tongue lashing I'll never forget. He said if I didn't want to work, I should get down off the mountain. And that work was a man's saving grace. It changed my way of thinking about work, and I vowed I'd never again be a slacker.

<u>*I'm embarrassed to admit once again to my immaturity and lack of social conscience. At the time, I felt privileged to be part of harvesting those majestic giant fir trees in Oregon; never realizing it took **hundreds** of years for them to grow to the size as large as they were.*</u>

<u>*But…that's where I was at then.*</u>
<u>*Bill and I even worked for a short while hookah diving for abalone off the windward side of Catalina Island in California.*</u>

Again, it was great money! It was the early sixties and a means to an end. We did what we could do for travel money, never dreaming that by harvesting too many abalone we were upsetting the underwater ecological balance in the pristine area.

We would work for a while and travel for a while; work a while, travel a while. It was a great lifestyle when we were young (and dumb).

*   *   *   *   *

The short periods of reminiscing and sleep were interrupted by acute "attacks" of itching. I would bolt upright at the waist and find myself feverishly scratching the bites and listening to the squeaking rhythm of the bamboo bed. Only the thought of awakening Frenchy curtailed the continuous scratching. Cigarettes were plentiful – though horrible tasting. But I smoked one after another in an effort to soothe my nervous body and vagrant mind.

I entertained the idea, and even tried once, to burn the more irritated areas of my ankles with embers of the lit cigarette hoping to stop the itching. But it didn't work. Nothing worked! Only the passage of time mattered.

*   *   *   *   *

After breakfast I talked with the foreman hoping to gain information about our position on the map. Much to my dismay he was unable to tell me, or show me, where on the map the camp was located. He only knew we were at a fork in the Canazas River where I took the bath last night. As there were as many as ten forks in the Canazas on the map, it was anybody's guess which one.

My spirits were dampened knowing the Chucunaque was still a long distance off. But the foreman, even though he didn't know how to read a map, knew of a trail leading to the great Chucunaque. He also knew there was no truck road going there, but added Frenchy was driving to Santa Fe later in the afternoon and would drop me off at the trailhead leading to the Chucunaque River. It was about forty-five minutes away riding the truck.

I asked him about how the trucks and equipment managed to get this far into the jungle. First, he said, his company shipped the bulldozer, crane, and trucks by boat to Santa Fe along the Pacific coastline from Panama City. Slowly they cut and bulldozed their way into the jungle until they got to the Rio Canazas. Over time, they floated logs down the river or shipped them by truck; a lot of teak and some balsa heading for the mills.

Possessed with this vague information, I had begun to assess my situation. I traveled around a hundred miles since leaving Jenene, had three remaining cans of C-rations (one of bread), and was in reasonably good health; except for the infected tick and chigger bites. Mentally, my will and determination was stronger than ever to make it through the Darien and into Colombia.

The Rio Chucunaque was, of course, my next immediate goal. From there I hoped to get to the coveted village of El Real; one way or the other. Once there, I was confident of getting boat transportation up river to Paya; the little village only five miles from the Colombian border.

It all sounded so easy...

*   *   *   *   *

The truck started its gas run - on time - at three o'clock. With Frenchy manhandling the steering wheel and feverishly shifting through the many gears, we bounced slowly down the uneven road.

After about forty minutes, he brought the truck to a stop in a whirl of dust. On the left side of the road, an eighteen by six inch cardboard sign stuck on a peg read: "CHUCUNAQUE". It was handwritten and underlined with an arrow pointing east. The sign gave me hope, as if many people had walked the trail many times before. I assumed the path would be an easy one to follow.

Frenchy climbed off the truck and with one arm over my shoulder and the other pointing down the trail, described an old abandoned campsite straight ahead after two hours of walking. He tried to emphasize the importance of sleeping there for the night. The Chucunaque, he assured me, would be within reach the following day. Or at least, that's what I *thought* he said.

As a parting gesture of our friendship, he handed me four oranges. I accepted them, but with some reluctance because I knew the members of the logging camp had very little extra food. Thanking him, I apologized for not being able to offer something in return for the accommodations, hospitality, and rides given to me by the camp.

He only laughed and said he only wanted to do more to help me. I said goodbye, and again thanked him and asked him to relay my thanks to all the men at the camp.

Standing next to the "CHUCUNAQUE" sign, I listened to the empty gasoline barrels rattling around the back of the truck as it disappeared down the jungle road in a storm of dust. I peered at the sign, noted how insecurely it was stuck in the ground, shook my head in bewildered disbelief, and started walking down the grassy trail.

*   *   *   *   *

Having eaten three good meals in the last twenty-four hours, my energy had been restored and my body felt strong. The trail was nearly truck-wide with only boot-high grass and easy going. If the trail remained this way, and if I could maintain a fast pace, there should be no difficulty reaching the abandoned campsite within the next two hours. And with the anticipation of reaching the Chucunaque River the next day, I drank from the canteen without hesitation.

I walked over the soft grass without stopping for what seemed more than two hours. But with no sign of a campsite, I just kept walking.

Eventually my movements were reduced to cautious stepping as the light of day was disappearing. Soon the maze of distorted tree-tops could barely be seen against the reddish sky, and then I was surrounded by the formlessness of an ignoble grey. Still I continued walking forward, slowly, trying to find the purported campsite.

I feared the proliferation of jungle vegetation could have overgrown *any* campsite after a *single* rainy season, but hoped upon hope it would be within the next few steps. Due to jungle conditions I had probably walked right past it.

Considered the biggest folly and a cardinal sin in exploration, I had walked into the darkness of night. And, not knowing exactly what the campsite looked like, my eyes strained to see the gap between the black walls of the forest and the uneven surface of the ground before me. Arms outstretched and boot tips gliding forward, I was literally feeling my way through the jungle; stumbling over clumps of mud and weeds a few feet at a time.

As could be expected, I tripped, fell forward, and awkwardly hit the ground with a dull thud. I felt a sharp jabbing pain in my left rib cage. The floundering machete had rammed into the soft dirt, blade first, as the handle cracked into my ribs; knocking the wind out of me

Gasping for breath, I then felt the warm stickiness of blood in the palm of my left hand. While attempting to cushion the fall, my left hand apparently slid along the sharpened edge of the machete's blade and caused a deep two inch cut near the thumb. Knowing the nearly emptied first-aid kit offered little; I tore a narrow strip of cloth off the bottom of my shirt and wrapped it around my hand to stop the bleeding. All of this happened in the darkness of night.

Far off in the distance I heard the ominous growling of an animal. It sounded as if it was a large animal, and the sounds were getting closer.

Confusion reigned.

As if a stroke of brilliance, I decided enough progress was made for one day – or night – and started to make camp. Feeling around in the saddle bags, I found a pack of matches and made a half-hearted attempt at a fire. Most of the kindling was damp or moss covered, so it wasn't much of a fire; and, I had wasted a lot of matches. But it did afford enough light to get the hammock strung between two solid trees.

I had often thought I could go through the ritual of preparing for camp blindfolded. Now it was coming true. With the fire out and only the sparse light of the stars, I managed to get the saddle bags hooked on a tree and myself safely in the hammock; machete within easy reach beside the hammock.

The still night air was buffeted by the frequent cries of the prowling animal heard earlier. As if a groan of anguish, the sounds went from a low pitch to a high pitch, and back to low. Sometimes the growls seemed near, and then far away. Slowly I realized the moans were definitely gravitating toward the smoky fire and my human scent.

As the growling became closer, I nervously shifted positions in the hammock and reached outside the mosquito netting for the machete and pulled it inside.

Suddenly I saw two round yellow eyes staring my way through the dark screen of uneven foliage. Only three or four feet from the front of the hammock and my bootless feet, they appeared fixated and piercing.

I was horror stricken!

Not knowing what to do and in complete shock, I mentally and physically froze. But adrenaline started pumping.

I didn't want to risk throwing the machete because of the possibility of losing it; and be without any protection.

Instinctively, I slowly and silently moved my right hand outside the mosquito net toward the ground until my fingers felt the dampness of the organic debris on the jungle floor. Like a burglar I groped through the nearby layers of dead leaves and twigs, looking for a rock; anything large enough to throw at the threatening menace before me.

Finally, in desperation, I thrust my fingers deep into the soft earth and grabbed a handful of whatever was there – dirt, stones, and leaves. In slow motion I pulled back my right arm while holding up the mosquito net with the left and, with all my might, hurled the fist full of stuff into the darkness at the yellow eyes before me.

At the same time, I let out this blood curdling scream at the top of my voice. It even hurt <u>my</u> ears.

The shrill sounding voice in the otherwise silent night probably frightened me more than the animal. But my scream was followed by a frenetic scampering of the animal heading in the opposite direction. The animal never returned, so the danger was over for now.

*   *   *   *   *

At first light, I arose with high hopes of reaching the Chucunaque before noon. For nourishment I ate an orange, the can of bread, and drank a large mouthful of water; leaving two cans of C-ration food, two very ripe oranges, and half a canteen of water. Fortunately, the jar of Halizone contained plenty of tablets for purifying any water I might find.

Preoccupied with survival, I set off down the trail longing for the sights and sounds of civilization.

Two hours of walking led me to the abandoned loggers' campsite – off to the right, just like Frenchy said. But no way would I have reached it last night. And even if I had walked that distance, the campsite was far enough off to the side of the trail that without doubt I would have missed it.

I thoroughly searched the whole campsite, looking for something of value. But nothing of value was there; only four broken-down bamboo huts and a central fireplace. A few rusted tin cans and several empty wine bottles were strewn around.

The fact that it took nearly seven hours of continuous walking to reach the abandoned campsite validated a growing suspicion that nobody, the Cuna, the loggers, or the missionaries were experts on the geography of the Darien Jungle. Each of them knew well their own areas. But once outside their perimeter, they were only guessing. This validated the need to proceed with caution when getting advice or information about directions in the jungle from Panamanians or the Cuna – *anyone*!

I left the old campsite in a mild state of disgust, and once again headed down the trail in a general easterly direction.

My skills and techniques of living in the jungle and walking the trails had greatly improved since my blind entrance those first few days. However, Mother nature had various and sundry ways of camouflaging and masking a jungle path.

A funny thing happened this morning along the path.

I ran into 4 Cuna men who seemed to be sweeping and clearing the path like municipal street cleaners. Or maybe they were making a new path. We saw each other and stopped everything. They looked at me and I looked at them. "What do we do now?" seemed to be on everyone's mind. I completely forgot the few Cuna words I was learning and they couldn't or wouldn't speak Spanish. Don't know why, but I got my shaving kit out of the saddle bags and got out the 2-sided mirror and offered it to the Cuna I thought was in charge. He looked at himself in the mirror, turned it over and looked into the magnified side, and let out a shrill yelp while hopping several inches off the ground. He threw the mirror to one of the other men, and he to the next, until each saw himself on both sides. Each responded with a similar yelp and a hop off the ground.

When they saw me laugh, they realized their own silliness and began smiling; and the ice was broken. I repeated the word "Chucunaque and used body language as if questioning "where?". They pointed in the direction I was going, and said something I couldn't understand. I gave them the mirror (while keeping a small flat one), waved goodbye and continued down the path; still chuckling to myself.

It was a brief but vivid encounter.

Sail ants traveled their own paths when transporting their neatly cut pieces of green leaf from its source to their homes. In the process they carved a clean narrow path out of the debris-covered jungle floor down to the bare earth. Millions of these mighty insects travel thousands of yards in many directions cutting and carrying their fresh green piece of leaf, always much larger and heavier than their body weight. The problem was an old ant path could be easily mistaken for the actual or man-made path. Often there were many to choose from in a crisscrossing pattern. In areas of heavy ant habitation I made the mistake of following an old ant trail over and over again, causing me a lot of backtracking. It was literally like taking two steps forward and one step backward.

Then too, the scores of dried creek beds left empty by the winter drought, had to be crossed. Torrential rains had swollen the banks of the creek beds, sweeping away dead vegetation leaving a clean stretch of soil. The original trail was often difficult to find after stumbling and bumbling to the other side. There were literally hundreds of deviations on the trail for every mile of forward progress. The fallen trees, slippery branches, impenetrable patches of undergrowth and minor trails leading to a long-forgotten attempt at home building all inadvertently helped me overcome a deep-seated rebelliousness and conform to the complexities of the living jungle.

Change or die! Not much of a choice here.

I was *forced* to keep my eyes focused on the ground. I was *required* to watch my feet stepping forward. I *needed* quick glances twenty or thirty feet forward. It was *necessary* to occasionally stop and catch my breath; to look at the surroundings; to look back from whence I came.

I had very little time to actually *think* of my situation and the prison-like containment; only the immediate environment invaded my conscience as an occasional foggy green blur. Sometimes the trail would be easy. Then suddenly as if metamorphosed into a flea on a shabby dog I would find myself surrounded by thousands of giant hair-like plants tugging, stabbing, scratching, and pulling at my irregular body.

I had to stop.

*   *   *   *   *

The following morning I awoke and wrote down this poem.

On The Path

The light of morning compels,
get ready, get set, adventure.
The first steps piercing straight ahead
the wonders of the world inside.

Stumbling with a fierce recovery,
focus on doubts and darkness.
I'm somewhere on the path,
an unknown leaf braises my skin.

A vision of the future anticipated,
a quick return to the cathedral.
Traversing holes, hunger, and pain,
but hey, it's the path of adventure.

To answer the why this lust,
will not stop the incessant desire.
Sometimes filling a simple need to *be*,
but perforce requiring the action to *do*.

Deviation to the right, deviation left,
sometimes yes, sometimes *nada*.

Determination will get me there,
a matter of time, a character sincere.

One step in before the other,
many others yet I must go.
There's something primal for all,
each step a creative beginning.

Then, the sweetness of reversion
the joy of love's remembrance.
A pause on the trails' supremacy
before the excitement returns.

Again in motion, uncertainty saturates,
asking of the struggle, will ever ease.
Trail without end, just a beginning;
trail inside a trail, secure in eternity.

The wonder of where it leads,
nagging and tearing, sweating, swearing.
Layered in the firmness of knowing,
walking, treading the omnipotent trail.

The immediate path before me
captured the vision of each choices.
Occasionally another future peek,
rarely a backward glance of lessons.

Lonely, there are others along the way
but unseen and on parallel paths.
Is there anybody here to share,
this adventure of the path?

The colorless dusk fraught with dreams,
clearing a spot, lay my weary head.

Setting aside the travails of the day,
the splendor of hope for trails to come.

*   *   *   *   *

I was in my usual mode of watching one foot go before
the other when there appeared a gradual clearing of the trees. It
was about mid-day and I'd been on the trail for nearly six hours.
My body was sodden with sweat but my spirits were rising.
Anticipating the first signs of the Chucunaque, my pace
quickened. The longing for the security of cool river water
lowered the pangs of hunger and thirst; and my filthy body…

My hopes were raised and my range of vision increased.
Soon trees disappeared completely and were replaced with eight
and ten feet tall sun-tarnished blades of grass. Dozens of would-
be paths intercepted the main trail going in every direction; each
point of the compass. Without the comfort of the overhanging
trees and vines I was disoriented and confused.

But it barely slowed my pace. I kept pushing forward.

My hope was to stay on the well-used trail leading in a
gradual downward slope into what appeared to be a basin. With
such a drastic change in the jungle terrain, something was near at
hand.

The high hopes and lofty anticipations quickly collapsed
when I saw a dilapidated thatched-roof hut beside a dried-out
creek or river bed. I knew at once this basin, nearly void of water,
could not possibly be the mighty Chucunaque River everyone
talked about. Just another abandoned logging site, I guessed.

Surveying the flat bushy jungle from the top of the bank, I
traced the would-be course of the empty creek. My eyes quickly
focused on several pools of stagnant water at different spots;
reflecting the sky above. Wanting to investigate, I unloaded the
equipment and hurried down the soft earthen bank toward the
first oval of water.

Before I got half-way down the hill the sight of a spirally
patch of thin vines lying scattered on the ground stopped me dead

in my tracks. Attached were large green melons. What luck! I could hardly believe my eyes! They looked like ordinary watermelons, only slightly smaller, with thin jagged streaks of dull yellow stretching down their length. They appeared edible; almost domesticated.

In a sweet dilemma, I hesitated for a long moment chaffed by the dual needs of thirst and hunger.

The food would wait!

I bounded down the last portion of the creek bank to the first pool of water anticipating some *real* water.

The vine water, while keeping me alive, had become too brackish and barely palatable.

The water in the pool, though stilled and slightly murky, was cool to the touch and smelled okay. Splashing some on my face, I noticed a few minnows or tadpoles darting about in apparent despair. The sight of life in the pond catalyzed my desire of drinking the water.

In one breath I gulped down the remaining canteen water and knew the water purification tablets would make the liquid suitable for drinking.

Filling the plastic canteen, I dropped in two of the Halizone tablets and loosely replaced the cap. Following the instructions on the label, I waited five minutes and shook the canteen vigorously so a small amount of water could leak through the cap and disinfect the upper surface of the canteen where my lips would touch. But I still had to wait thirty minutes before the Halazone completed its task of killing any and all germs in the water.

I had gone through this process many times, but knowing this water to be stagnant made me doubly conscious of following the instructions.

Twisting on the canteen cap I retraced my steps to the melon patch. From the assortment of the not-too-ripe to the already-rotten melons, one gave the appearance of being ripe and ready to eat. Pulling off the stem I carried it to the hut and began cutting it into halves and then into quarters. Cleaning out as many seeds as my impatience would allow, I cut the fourths into eights, sprinkled them with C-ration salt, and began a gorging frenzy.

The flesh was solid and crunchy to chew, much like an un-ripened cantaloupe, and had a rather thick bitter taste that made me click my tongue against the top of my mouth. But it pacified the gnawing in my stomach; so I ate the whole melon.

But one was enough! I couldn't eat another because my stomach had bloated and experienced waves of cramps. The air suddenly seemed hotter and heavier than usual, and breathing came only with an effort. My forehead started to sweat profusely; the roof of the hut swirled around and around.

Too much water and un-ripened and un-chewed melon filled my stomach. I was forced to lean over the hand-rail of the hut and vomit until my stomach was once again empty. Weakened, I sat down on the floor and leaned my back against a corner wall. Though I couldn't see it, I felt the radiating heat of the overhead sun penetrating the roof. The sounds of the jungle were suddenly silent; only a few promiscuous mosquitoes bopping around my head with their irritable buzz. An acidic taste remained in my saliva, as sweat poured slowly from every open pore. My unfocused eyes stared off into the distant trees; my mind without depth of thought.

I tried to cheer myself in reminiscence.

How wonderful was the time of early adolescence, before the harshness and hardships of the reality of life became burdensome. Especially wonderful were the summer days when I and the gang could travel "somewhere"; go wherever we liked and do whatever we wanted. We'd go to the river, the quarry, a farm, into the woods. All the kids in our gang had great names, like: Ticky, Bumper, Pork, Cod-ball, Boots, and some unmentionables. We didn't care for conventionality; our hair was usually in serious need of a trim; our socks were often

worn through at the heels; and with shoes, we competed with who had the biggest holes in the sole and covered the hole from the inside with a piece of cardboard. We ran barefoot at the first opportunity.

I wonder what they're doing now. I heard Bumper got married and had a bunch of kids. Ticky went to jail again before finally getting a good life with a great wife and kids. Cod-ball became a cop. Can you believe that – a cop? Never heard much about Pork, he was always a bit of a mystery. Boots was older and never really part of us. He was always in a fight, so he's probably lucky to still be alive.

Father MacDonald's farm was our favorite. We loved hitchhiking the 4 or 5 miles down Route 30 to get there because it was more fun than walking; always something different happened; always someone new talking to us.

I never did know how big it was but the priests and nuns who ran it also taught in the school on the hill next to the farm. After a while, they tried to stop us from coming on, but that only made it more fun. Sometimes we'd swear at the nuns, but not the priests because they ran too fast. We'd run through the hills, eat their sweet corn off the stalks, have all the green apples we wanted, and pick their cherries. We drank water from the creek or pumped water from their well. The most fun was playing in the barn. We'd have hay fights, chase the cows and try to milk them, throw stones at the pigeons, and just generally raise hell. All this while trying to not get caught. None of us ever did get caught, but some other kids from town did and were arrested, put on probation, and had to pay a big fine. I'm sure the priests and nuns said a blessing when the fall and winter rolled around. What we did was wrong, we knew, but...we were just a bunch of undisciplined kids.

I was the only one who didn't have a father. Ticky's mother died early, Pork's dad would slap him upside the head for no reason at all, Bumper came from a pretty good family but there were a lot of them, Cod-ball's parents were both remarried, and Boots never talked about his family. Being fatherless, I used to watch them closely and try to see how we were different. I remember once a little girl liked me and invited us to her birthday party, but her mother wouldn't let me come because "He didn't come from a good family." I try not to think much about those incidents, but I love to think about those sunny summer days on the farm, and wonder whatever happened to the guys. Were they happy and satisfied with their lives?

At the moment, all I had was a miserable upset stomach and a swarm of mosquitoes surrounding my head. But the day-dreaming rest marginally settled my stomach and brought me back to the unpleasant realities of the moment.

It was March 2nd, 1965, and I was in the middle of the Darien Jungle trying to get to the Chucunaque River. I had just vomited and a slight stomach cramp remained. There were about four hours of daylight remaining, so I decided to drink some of the Halizone-cleansed water and get back on the trail. Because the melon had given me the cramps I didn't want to carry any with me; plus the added weight was an unnecessary burden that would undoubtedly slow me down. I moved on.

But finding the main trail, or any trail for that matter, was easier said than done.

After aimlessly wandering around near the old campsite for half an hour, I caught a glimpse of a small path heading in an easterly direction. Once "inside" the montage of jungle growth, it soon became obvious the trail would be difficult. An unusually large number of fallen trees obstructed the trail; and the undergrowth was thick to an extreme. Like an ancient soldier in battle, I hacked and sliced at the aggressive and groping bush. The machete waved methodically before me in continuous symmetry. Only an occasional metallic clang of the machete striking a hard wooden branch broke the monotonous swiping and swooshing sound of the blade as the jungle sword whizzed through the air slashing the moist plants.

Several times I was forced to stop and use my trusty file to again hone the machete's blade into carving sharpness. I sat on a rotten log, hunched over the machete pushing the file over the edge with sweat dribbling down from my hairy face and onto the blade in rhythmic drops.

Then I noticed the wetness on my right pant-leg. Automatically reaching for the canteen, it was obvious I failed to fully tighten the cap. It was loose! Somehow I had forgotten to tighten it properly after the last filling, and it had been slowly leaking ever since. Nearly half of the water had been wasted because of a lack of discipline. I vowed to drink no more water until the following day.

Grudgingly, I continued through the natural greenhouse thickness.

The terrain took a turn for the worse (again), and became almost swamp- like. An eerie feeling came over me as I entered this low area. The air was thick and stifled all sounds. The surrounding green plants were dull and drab, and emitted a foul odor. The thickness of the overhead trees permitted no sunlight through. The trail was soggy with thick black soil gushing over the tops of my boots like crude oil.

Every twenty or thirty yards was a dried creek bed equally black and soft. The jungle brush was now replaced by a pot-like plant whose stems sprouted long thick blades of juicy leaves of brass, but much larger than a man. The problem was each blade of grass was armed with extra long cactus-like thorns spiking out every inch or so down the seven-foot long leaves. To the touch, each was as sharp as a cat's claw and strong as the teeth of a dog. When sliced at a good angle, the blades were easy to cut and quickly fell to the ground.

The quasi-trail came to a stunning end at an empty creek bed. In front of me was a wall of these intimidating forbidding plants, towering above with their thorny needles poking out in every direction. In desperation I followed the creek bed in each direction for at least a hundred yards, hoping to avoid the catastrophic thorns and trying to find an easier passage. But there was nothing. The only way was to hack my way through.

Using a tall tree several hundred feet in front of me as a guiding position, the ferrous hacking began. With each blow of the machete, four or five stalks fell at my feet, and each of them had to be cut into small pieces. The jagged thorns pricked at my skin, tugged at my clothing, and even penetrated the material of my boots. Blow after blow I pulverized each stalk into smaller pieces until I was able to make an exaggerated step over the pile of sticky fiber.

The stems were all around. I had to fight for each step forward. A claustrophobic fear gripped me. I was bending, twisting, and contorting my body into unbelievable shapes and positions. But no matter how cautious or athletic were the moves, some thorns penetrated my skin somewhere on my body. Each injection caused me to recoil, which caused me to move away, which caused me to get pricked again; and on and on.

Like a prisoner obsessed with freedom, I sliced at every nearby plant forcing my way forward aiming for that lonely tree seen in the distance. I was fighting for my life, fighting for freedom from this hell hole of nature that was tearing at me with each movement; trying to consume me. I craved the simple pleasure of standing upright walking and to swing my limbs back and forth unobstructed.

Reaching the solitary tree, I fell to the ground in exhausted agitation. The soiled bandage covering the cut from yesterday was ripped open and displayed additional deep scratches. Salty sweat ran down my arm and into the many wounds; stinging with each drop. A dangerous scratch close to my left eye twitched uncontrollably.

Primal fear again took command and forced me to continue; or be mauled to death by these green monsters. Plus, thoughts of the approaching darkness added to the motivation.

Without consulting the compass, I resumed the cutting without caring in which direction I was going – only to higher ground devoid of these overwhelming plants. The machete blade dulled, and I was in no position to sharpen it. Forgetting my bleeding hand I fought my way forward. Each step was like my recurring childhood nightmare. "Someone" or "something" was after me and I was running away. But no matter how hard or fast I tried to run, my legs would move only in slow motion as if the soles of my feet were covered with glue. Meanwhile, the monster was moving toward me, and getting closer. But, as with all dreams of insecurity, I always woke up before being captured.

No chance of waking out of *this* nightmare. This was real, and my temples throbbed like pounding pistons in a loud engine and my heart felt as if it were bursting out of my chest cavity. If only…

There were no second guesses – only perseverance.

The thickness of the blades eventually thinned into a hedge-like maze. Nearly "out" of the trapping jaws of the thorns, I chopped a path through the thinning plants to the top of the hill. Then I was able to chop for fifteen feet and walk unobstructed for maybe ten feet. These distances of walking without obstacles increased until I was completely out of the swamp area and again on high ground. It was the most difficult quarter mile I ever traveled!

Physically and emotionally shattered, I wanted to make camp early to avoid the confusion of rummaging in the dark like I had the night before. I unhesitatingly chose a spot for camp near an old fallen tree, cleared a few feet of ground, gathered firewood, and strung the hammock, all on the momentum of a still quickened pulse. I started a one-match fire using my last match and slumped to the ground on the poncho to calm down and absorb the warm rays of the flickering fire.

I saturated my handkerchief with as little canteen water as possible, squeezed the excess water into my mouth, cheating on my vow of not drinking until tomorrow, and proceeded to cleanse my bloody hands, arms, and legs; while trying to sooth my ruffled emotions. Afterward, I threw it in the already brightly burning fire.

Gradually, the mesmerizing effect of the orange flames piercing the black air captivated my eyes and threw my torpid mind into thoughtfulness.

Well, I did it again! Put myself in prison. Instead of green bars and cement, this time it was a jungle and deprivation. G-1449 was my number there - the State Youth Facility in Camp Hill, Pennsylvania; just a fancy name for a prison. I was in a cell with bars. We called it "White" Hill; I don't know why. 1956 is when I went in. Sixteen months, six days, and 10 hours I got out. "G" was the letter for my cell-block. "H" cell-block was for the blacks. Things were segregated then. I remember, each cell-block had four tiers and each tier had a "Belt". The Belt was picked by the guards because he was the biggest baddist guy on a tier of maybe 50 kids. It was their job to keep us all in line; they did most of the disciplinary work of the guards. The big perk of being a Belt was that you spent almost no time in your cell, except to sleep at night and you had the other 3 Belts and all the guards behind you. If anyone fell out of line while in the cell-block, the Belts held a Kangaroo Court on the back stairwell. Nobody heard or saw anything. Few fell out of line.

It was hard times – no doubt; lonely, intimidating, demoralizing. Twice I ended up on the "bench" (first level of discipline). Had my jaw socket damaged. Took a kidney shot to the back that dropped me to the floor and caused me to piss blood. Kissed a guy once. But never got punked.

And, most importantly, I never went back. Many of the guys I knew did.

I tossed another piece of wood on the fire.

Except for a broken-down motorcycle I would never see again, I was carrying everything I possessed: the saddle-bags, hammock and mosquito net, machete, a few books, an extra shirt, shaving kit, snakebite kit, an old pair of sneakers, two cans of C-rations, and an orange; and found a few more fish hooks on the bottom. Also, I had a hundred dollars in American Express Travelers check and my passport.

*What drives me on? What drives **anyone** on? It's got to be more complex than...than what?*

*I was never big on the Church thing; I went only because I had to. But the notion of the existence or non-existence of God always captured my imagination and stimulated me toward higher thinking. And people a lot smarter than me have told me their views both for and against. But here I am, 26 years old, sitting alone in the middle of the jungle with nobody to influence me either way, what do **I** believe about God? I could easily die at any moment. Would some part of me continue, or is this it? It's hard to imagine an **end**. **Change** yes, but an **end**? I don't think so.*

*If we are only material beings, by what method do we know that? How can we be conscious of that fact? How can a material **thing** be aware that it is only material? Does a tree know it's a tree? I don't know. Maybe because I am close to death I'm getting closer to believing in God. Like afterlife insurance. But I always liked Jesus. Some of the stories told about him...I'm not too sure of. I guess I was always a little afraid of believing in God. If I did, it would make me do things another way or do things I really didn't want to do. But considering my ridiculous position here and now, that doesn't sound so bad.*

Still uncomfortable in the dampness, I turned away from the fire to dry the backside of my clothing.

The torment of the bug bites was returning. Each movement of my body produced pain. All of my energies were again pointed toward survival. This carnivorous jungle beast was consuming me, bit by bit. As with each night, I calculated how much food and water my body had received this day; while hoping for some real food for tomorrow. Why, why was I so preoccupied with survival; in this life and the next?

Still aching and confused, I slipped my body under the mosquito net and swung on the hammock; hoping for the balm of sleep.

*   *   *   *   *

In between the sudden itching attacks and cigarette smoking, I managed a little sleep. I remembered a dream: I was walking on a smooth plane with comfortable clothes, fresh air, and light above – but somehow it wasn't skylight. The surface of the plane was of smooth dark glass, or marble, or plastic. In the distance was a brilliant gleaming green tree with what looked like shiny fruit on it. A small pond of mirror-like water was nearby. Everything was immaculate; no dirt, dust, or slime. Like a ballet dancer, I was gliding through the air with only half-gravity holding me down. I was going to the tree. I began to hasten with anticipation, but the tree always remained at the same distance. No matter how high or far or fast I went, it wouldn't come any closer. Frustrated, my jumping stopped. Then, with palms turned inward, I lowered my head and continued walking toward the tree in sullen resignation.

Chapter 6

The morning after the dream I woke up with cracked and bleeding lips. Stomach contractions and pangs had become less frequent. And the night's rest did little to ease the feeling that my body had been hit by a fast moving car.

Nonetheless, I habitually undressed to pick and scrape the ticks and chiggers off my lower body. A feeling of despondency overcame me as I put on the dank, dirty, smelly clothes. Apathetically, I ordered myself to put on the pants, and the boots, now the shirt, jacket, and the hat too. As if sculptured to my body, each item easily slides into position. Listlessly I moved about preparing to get back on the trail, yet thinking of ways to avoid it.

It would have been easy to just stay there and die. I was on no particular trail without any particular landmarks in sight; and really, I was going nowhere. My bones would never be found. But, *ha*, that would have been the easy way out!

If I am going to die, life will have to be pulled from me!

Already feeling drained and not wanting to pursue burning philosophical questions, I sat down on the sleeping roll and began eating my last orange. It was a large wonderful specimen, a little on the soft side. Full of juice, it momentarily satisfied my body; even though the acidic juice burned my cracked lips.

Then like an addiction, my mind was re-ignited. A body was like a bank account: you put some in and you take some out. If you take out more than you put in – bad things will happen; even death. I would suppose it was the same with the intellect. I didn't know if our higher consciousness was attributed to God, but assumed it to be of the same pattern. I didn't remember who said it, but liked the quote: "Money cannot love." I thought a lot, but was running out of funds to put in my bank account, and had nobody to love.

*   *   *   *   *

To stop the endless procession of thoughts, I painstakingly settled the saddle-bags and sleeping roll on my now thinning shoulder muscles. I stepped back onto the jungle path with the compass in my left hand and the machete in the right, heading in a generally easterly direction.

My movements were slow and deliberate, almost casual. The sense of urgency was gone; it had been beaten into passivity. Or was it an outward display of adjusting to the will and the ways of my Supreme Overseer – the jungle? It was almost as if yesterday's torture chamber of thorns was a climax of the Darien's aggressiveness of "testing" me, and I was now "accepted" as a part. Maybe the rest of the journey would be "down hill".

Laboriously, I began traveling hundreds of yards in either direction in an effort to avoid obstacles. The bulldozing method used in the last few days obviously wasn't working. I needed to conserve energy.

The burning passion to make it through the Darien Jungle into South America had dwindled until only a few embers of pink remained. The constant abuse of my body and the daily strain of survival had dampened the fire until it no longer mattered. Nothing mattered.

*   *   *   *   *

Near mid-day, a definite commotion among the loft branches of the trees broke the usual sounds of the jungle. As I looked up I saw a group of about twenty or twenty-five monkeys jumping and leaping from the myriad of vines and branches away from the intruding sounds that had entered their sacred world. The harsh sounds of my footsteps and slicing machete put them on hyper alert.

Then the screams started!

At first only a steady tempo of shrieking yelps and rustling branches reached my ears. But once they saw my alien body movements coming through the brush below, the entire group sensed danger at the same instant. The jungle quickly came alive with their high pitched squealing and loud scampering through the trees. Their continuous atonal wails mounted to nearly unbearable heights as they sprang from tree to tree in frenzied disorder to escape their unwanted intruder.

They were the first monkeys I'd seen since entering the Darien and, though ear deafening, were intriguing and fun to watch. I never felt threatened.

*I discovered later they were, in fact, **howler** monkeys. After the blue whales, they are the loudest of all animal creatures on earth.*

First of all, they were *huge;* some looked to be three or four feet tall. They were furry and ranged in color from light brown to black. Then, I thought they had *three* legs when as I saw them hanging and swinging from the tree branches. But the "third leg" was actually a very thick tail, equally as round as their legs.

I had been led to an area of thinned-out trees, and as I was watching my step I saw a very large Brazilian Ivory nut lying on the ground. I could hardly believe my eyes. What a combination: long-tailed monkeys and three-sided nuts.

Of course I also found out later, the howler monkeys are vegetarians and fed primarily on leaves, and supplementing their diet with fruits, nuts, and maggots.

I had no idea from where the nut came and didn't care, but proceeded with the nervous task of cracking open the hard outer shell. Soon, and sure enough, inside was a perfectly formed – ready to eat – ivory colored nut. It was beautiful! I placed the whole nut inside my mouth to be sure to not lose one grain of nutrition, and slowly bit off, chewed thoroughly, and swallowed one small portion at a time until the entire contents settled comfortably inside my stomach.

Intently I looked around for more, but didn't find any.

A nearby fallen log proved to be a good rest stop to allow my good fortune to digest. Ironically, the monkeys seemed to have made a three-hundred and sixty degree turn because they were now at nearly the same angle as before when I found the nut; not too far away.

I wondered if they would allow me to get closer. So, head held high, I cautiously walked in their general direction. Before I realized what was happening, a small opening in the jungle maze was before me. Pumped with adrenalin and hoping for the best, I explored the immediate area. The earth looked freshly overturned and mixed with broken tree limbs and twisted roots. In the soft dirt were definite impressions of tracks of some type; likely the tracks of a bulldozer. The clearing was also littered with tree stumps and short pieces of what smelled like cedar logs mixed with many types of broken branches; obvious victims of man-made machinery.

The clearing was circular – similar to the one near the campsite on the Rio Canazas – with a single towering mutilated tree near the center. The circling tracks funneled into what appeared to be a well-used <u>road</u>. My heart leaped in disbelief at such luck. Soon I was standing in the middle of yet *another* road! that appeared freshly cut and well used. The down-side was it ran in a north-to-south direction instead of easterly.

The Rio Chucunaque *had* to be near.

Guessing a northerly route would lead me to water, I headed up the road with thoughts of water floating in my head. The prospect of sighting another truck was, I knew, too much to hope for.

I started walking. The dusty road was lighted by rays of the mid-day sun puncturing through the overhead foliage. After a short distance the road led to an intersection; and then another intersection. Automatically at each crossroad I read and re-read the compass hoping for an easterly course. Sometimes it did, but always it followed to a dead-end where a bulldozer, for some unexplainable reason, stopped its forward motion leaving a three or four foot high mound of dirt.

This necessitated the agonizing ordeal of retracing my steps. Often a distance of two or three miles had to be retraced; sometimes actually stepping in the imprints the boots made previously.

From junction to junction I walked until the indecision and uncertainty became immobilizing. What little energy I had left was being uselessly wasted. I simply walked up a road to its end, turned around and walked back. It was so meaningless.

This is getting to be a little like the "Myth of Sisyphus". He was condemned (by some Greek gods) to rolling this rock up to the top of the mountain, watch it roll back down, then start rolling it back up again; over and over and over again.

Eventually I gave up hope of trying to solve the riddle of road maze and walked obediently on; following whatever natural instincts remained.

At an unusually low dip in the road I found a large pool of stagnant water in the bed of a once flourishing creek; another victim of the dry season. I stepped on the brittle moss covering the rocks and sat down for a rest and to refill my canteen. A light breeze increased the volume of trees and branches rubbing together almost melodically, hastening a desire to bathe; and, a chance to temporarily rid myself of the nausea-inducing clothes.

The relish of popping the ticks between my fingernails had long since lost its novelty. Instead I simply scraped the knife over my legs until the ticks and chiggers peeled off. My legs were gradually beginning to show the swollen, septic signs of the many earlier bites. Only a few shreds of wool remained of the last pair of stockings. Somehow, I didn't care.

The physical hardships were being overshadowed by the internal anguish of mental fatigue and depression, which were severely compounded by the pangs of extreme loneliness. Interacting with the loggers was good, but with the language barrier... I really couldn't express myself in any range of complexities in the Spanish language. I craved humanity; to be elbow-to-elbow; to feel the multitudes around me. I wanted someone to talk with; someone to touch; to share; to dream with. I wanted someone, and I wanted everyone.

I wanted some gratification; to be entertained; to hear the rich fulfilling sounds of music; the taste of good food; the joy of humor; to see beautiful things.

But here and now there was nothing! I was completely restricted and dominated by the choking environment. Only the monotonous jungle sounds penetrated my senses: the persistent mosquito buzz; the mocking birds; the faint breeze; the sound of a falling palm leaf rattling its way to the ground. I could almost detect the faint sound of breathing.

After a cool bath, I dumped everything out of the saddle-bags with the hope of finding a few morsels of long-discarded food; even an old orange peeling or a few crumbs of stale bread. I pulled out my wallet hoping to find a picture of someone inadvertently stuck in an unused slot. But there was none; not one picture of *anyone*. How sad!

One can of noodles and one of beef-stew was all the food that remained. Each can glistened in the speckled sunlight as if an image of a pagan god. To eat or not to eat was the question. Was it sacrifice or self-forgetfulness? Either way, I could easily die soon.

Fear of starvation prompted me to toss the two cans of food into the saddle-bags and buckle them tightly; I discarded a few packages of salt on the rocks beside the water.

All the while, I had fantasies of entering a restaurant and ordering a very large filet mignon of Kobe beef – cooked medium to rare - with mushrooms, baked potato stuffed with cream cheese and a green salad served with Roquefort dressing; and a frosty Heineken beer served in a large thick glass.

Should I drink "just one" or not? I <u>do</u> have a problem.

Then there was dessert: dark chocolate ice cream covered with whipped cream and topped with fresh strawberries; or a milk shake, banana cream pie; or…

But all these fantasies would not fill my stomach now, so I slid on what was left of my stockings, delicately strapped the damp stinking boots around my swollen ankles and continued down the road.

*   *   *   *   *

My stamina became a wonder to me. I knew not from where the strength was coming. It seemed to require my last ounce of energy to just lift my boot the slightest fraction of an inch off the surface of the dusty road and move it forward. Forward, to the top of the next hill; then down. Going downhill, resisting the pull of gravity, was just as costly; if not more so. Somehow I remained in forward motion.

Where is the energy coming from? Where does _any_ energy come from? How do I keep moving? Why? Is it worth it?

The saddle-bag straps had, by this time, caused indentations in my shoulder muscles. On the left, where the mound of my left collar bone bulged, the skin was raw and red from the constant swaying of the bags. Often a small electric shock raced down my left side and back to my brain. The weight of the sleeping roll had rounded my shoulders until it was only with the utmost effort that I could fill my lungs or stand upright. It was as if I were on another planet with two or three times the gravitational pull as earth. My legs were heavy as lead, while my arms hung like lifeless chunks of beef suspended from my shoulders. I dared not raise the machete for fear of being unable to control its path or predetermine its destination.

Would it be possible to wander these abandoned roads forever – or until I died – never finding the Chucunaque? Never finding help or returning to civilization? Sure makes me wonder if I was pre-destined to perish in this jungle? Or was it because of my own damn dumb choices? I could die today, tonight, tomorrow, anytime. I just didn't care. I was no longer afraid of fear; of death; of anything.

I was nearing the end of what once felt like a pool of strength that was bottomless, and knew it.

*   *   *   *   *

Ever so slowly, I trudged down the road as if in slow-motion. The deep dust on the road splashed away from my steps as if stepping into a pool of water after a quiet rain. I felt as if I had finally reached the bottom of that once seemingly infinite pool of energy, flagrantly misused in the past.

In a bit of an epiphany, I suddenly realized I could no longer blame it on the jungle; the road parted the waves of foliage; I could no longer blame it on being without a father; I was an adult person now; I could no longer blame God (about whom I was uncertain) for my sorrows and misfortunes; a good God would not show favoritism. But there are rules to follow. I could not blame others. I had no one to blame but myself!

Then too, I could also take credit for my achievements; and revel in the glory of experiences past.

This realization provided me with motivation and energy to continue. But my body would not cooperate. The length of each step became shorter and shorter until forward progress completely stopped.

I just stood there for a while not knowing what to do next; not even certain I could do something. The sun was getting low and I could look directly into its burning conflagration without squinting. A pair of dark colored birds flew across the image of the sun; relaying their loud approval in repetitious calls. A large dried leaf scraped and pushed its way to the ground not far away.

Maybe the birds are showing me the way. Maybe it's just over the next hill. Perhaps, perhaps, perhaps. Perhaps what? What am I really looking for? Where is that vision, that bliss, Kerouac promised?

I still needed to see, and find out for myself, what was over the next hill.

Moving my left foot forward, I tried walking. But the moments of idleness were too long, and my stiffened knee suddenly buckled and I fell to the ground. I stuck out my left arm in an unsuccessful attempt to absorb the shock of the sudden fall. But my arm would not support the falling weight, and my left cheek struck the ground with a dull thump; drenching me in dust.

Time stood still; or perhaps was transcended. I lay there trying to count the brilliant spots bouncing before my eyes; close, and yet so far away. For no apparent reason, I stuck my tongue out until the tip of it was touching the road dust; amused at my nonchalance. I pushed my tongue to the roof of my already dry mouth to feel and taste the granules of dust.

But my cheek gave off a distracting burning sensation igniting that grand survival instinct. Slowly, I drew the sleeping roll across my body and rested my head upon it to relieve the pain of the bruised cheek.

My mind continued to function; though not very quickly. I knew I had to get off the jungle floor, or the insects would soon feast upon my body. Yet it would have been so easy to just lie there, head resting comfortably on the sleeping roll, watching the evening stars find their way through the cobalt blue sky; my mind searching for something meaningful.

I might have lain there forever, fondling abstractions, if my most hated and feared enemies – the insects - had not forced me into action. There were already several crawling on my face. Was there no escape from their interminable onslaught? I wanted to run, but could only flop over on my stomach, push myself up on my knees, and take a deep breath; and then another, and another.

Standing on my feet, I moved a few yards to the side of the road and unrolled the sleeping gear. In a slipshod manner, I managed to tie the hammock between two trees and hang the mosquito net. I completely undressed and slid into the hammock under the poncho with a sigh of relief; leaving everything strewn between the middle of the road and the hammock.

Lightly feeling my body, and at every little bump, I would dig my cracked and broken fingernails in my skin hoping to pull off as many ticks as possible. Then, thrusting my hand out from under the mosquito net, I flicked the insects into the darkened jungle. Sometimes it was only a scab from a previously infected bite I flicked away. My whole body felt as if it was crawling with ticks.

A little more than an hour had passed when suddenly I saw a blinding brightness passing between the trees. Like a strobe light it flashed directly into my eyes, blinding me until everything was unrecognizable.

Rolling out of the hammock, I stood up and stared, motionless like a deer. The deafening sound helped me realize a _truck_ was charging down the road. It stopped and was idling just in front of my array of dropped equipment.

Limping out of the trees toward the headlights, the riders were probably petrified at the sight of me. In their shining light, I appeared bone-thin with bleached white skin, and naked as the day I was born. My red beard had grown wild and scraggly, and dried blood covered much of my lower legs.

The voice of the driver was a little shaky as I approached the door-less cabin of the truck. To add to the confusion, I inexplicably forgot every word of Spanish ever learned, and only rapidly repeated in English: "food", "water", "help", and "take me with you", none of which they were able to comprehend.

Finally the word _"momento"_ filtered its way from my brain to my tongue; repeating it in rapid session for fear they would drive away without me. As quickly as my sapped strength allowed, I dressed and threw my gear together. Both the driver and the front seat passenger pointed me to the bed of the pick-up truck – with a wry smile. Also in the bed of the small truck sat four Panamanians with outstretched legs, staring in disbelief; too dumbfounded to open the tailgate.

The truck started bouncing down the road and a few words of Spanish returned to my vocabulary. I broke the silence and asked for food, but received only a look of perplexity in return. Confusion mounted as the front seat passenger proudly showed the packets of salt I had left behind, and he had found at the waterhole earlier. With a glowing face, he smiled broadly in the light from the dashboard, displaying a wide toothless smile.

I responded saying "Si." it was my salt packages. But added "No." it was not what I was trying to say. I was starving and nobody understood.

Only cigarettes were offered by rough black-skinned hands. Soon tiny sparks from tobacco ashes swirled past my eyes and into the passing scenery.

Eventually the truck slid to a stop after a twenty minute ride. We had arrived at what appeared to be their campsite, but I was unable to get off the truck unassisted. Things became emotionally charged when the men forcibly demanded I keep my gear on the truck. One of the men hooked me by the arm and led the way through a clump of trees and down a narrow path toward a small burning kerosene lamp sitting next to a large open fireplace. I was in no condition to resist.

It was a small campsite accommodating only six or eight men; all of whom I presumed were loggers. With the men from the truck, they crowded around me simultaneously speaking in rapid Spanish. It was impossible to fathom even one word of what they were trying to say.

After a few minutes, one of the men produced a small freshly baked loaf of bread and handed it to me. Even before I had a full grasp of the bread, I began tearing off big chunks of it and pushing it into my mouth; barely chewing before swallowing. Gracelessly, I plopped down next to the fire and proceeded to have a private banquet of baked bread. About midway through, someone handed me a large cup of steaming tea that tasted like the bark of a cinnamon tree. The feast was memorably delicious; interrupted only by an occasional gasp for air. Never had a simple loaf of bread tasted this good, had I drank a tea so satisfying. I consumed every last little crumb and every drop of the liquid.

Stomach bloated, mouth burnt, muscles aching, I leaned backward against a tree stump and relaxed into a state of supreme bliss; ignorant of what was happening around me.

The men watched in shock while shaking their heads in quiet disbelief. They shook me from my contented reverie by motioning it was time to return to the truck.

I had no idea where they were taking me. But after thanking the campsite men for the bread and tea, I sheepishly followed the guys back to the truck. We arranged ourselves on the bed of the truck and the vehicle once again continued down the dusty road in the darkness of the moonless night.

*   *   *   *   *

I suddenly felt very lazy and sleepy, even though I knew sleep would be impossible. Between the pounding bumps on the metallic truck bed and with the constant vibrations from the engine, I could only stare at the monotonous dust-covered trees and plants passing by.

My head dropped on my right shoulder allowing the cool air of the jungle night to buffet my face. I closed my eyes and allowed the passing air to funnel into my mouth creating a low howling sound of whistling in my ears.

The constant flapping of my hair, like the soft rhythmic tones of a clock, took me back to an earlier time and a previous place.

"__GET READY__" The piercing sound of those two words always sent an electric shock down my spine. I never got used to it; never. They were the words of the Jumpmaster when the red light next to the open door of the airplane came on; turned on by the pilot exactly five minutes before reaching the Drop Zone. This time it was my "cherry" jump – the __first__ jump a paratrooper makes __after__ getting the five jumps necessary for his wings after the completion of jump school. And, it was my first night jump! The tiny illuminating floor lights came on and I could see and smell the vomit near my boots sloshing up and down the grooves in the belly of the old Flying Box Car (C-119) aircraft as it flew the air. The smell was horrendous.

"__STAND UP__" As we stood up, I was ordered to the front of the stick because of the heavy GP (general purpose) pack strapped to my parachute harness. It contained a forty-five caliber machine gun, a tripod, and several boxes of ammunition; about one hundred pounds in all. Only the stick leader, a second lieutenant, was in front of me; a man I'd never

seen before. It had been a long flight from Pope Air Base beside Fort Bragg, North Carolina to near Fort Jackson, South Carolina. It had been a bumpy rider, and I too was beginning to feel nauseous; as the deafening wind screeched past the open door. It was February of 1959.

"HOOK UP" There was nothing tricky about this. Just a thick snap-hook to click onto the one inch thick cable running along the inside length of the mostly hollow plane. But it was something that had to be done – your life depended on it. I yanked on it three or four times to be sure it was secured. It was easy to see I was one of the shortest guys in the stick – maybe the shortest. So I never could understand why I was most always the one chosen for a GP; or other heavy-duty equipment. But I never dropped out of a march or run and always finished the rounds of calisthenics; and we always ran five miles every morning before breakfast. I was a private first class in the 82nd Airborne Division, 1st 503rd and damn proud of it.

"CHECK STATIC LINE" The static line is what pulled open your parachute. Every man had to check the static line of the man in front of him to be sure the fifteen foot nylon line connected to the cable in the airplane would unravel evenly and pull off the parachute pack allowing the main chute to open. This created a big trust factor between jumpers. You had to trust that person behind you that he would actually check your static line, and that it was packed correctly and ready to go. Focusing on small details like the rubber bands made me more queasy, and I was beginning to perspire. I was wondering whose name was written in the tiny notebook on my chute; and hoped they were sober enough when they did it.

"CHECK EQUIPMENT" At this point, we had to check our own harness straps and buckles for twists. And in my case, that the GP was snapped on properly. All buckles and straps were firmly fitted and straight. My chin strap was too tight causing the webbing inside the helmet to put pressure on the top of my crew-cut head. Of course, I double-checked the

reserve chute. It was my head I was worried about; things inside the aircraft were starting to spin, and I was desperately trying to hold back the vomit.

"SOUND OFF EQUIPMENT CHECK" Each person, from the back of the C-119 forward yelled "Ready" as loud as they could. The red light glared into my eyes. Would it never turn green? The jumpmaster looked at the Lieutenant stick leader in front of me; then looked at me, and smiled. He knew it was my cherry jump, that I was leaning on the GP, and not fully alert.

"STAND IN THE DOOR" Of all the commands this was the most meaningful; the fail/safe point. As the jumpmaster gave this order, we all shuffled forward a few steps. The Lieutenant stood with his body just inside the door, but with both hands pressing tightly against the outside; one foot halfway out. He looked confident. I, on the other hand, stuck my face under his left arm and into the air passing at a hundred and twenty miles an hour and proceeded to vomit my guts out.

"GO" Amid all the confusion, the light had turned green, and as I looked up the Lieutenant was gone – out the door. Everyone behind me was yelling "Go", "Go", "Go". And before I knew it, I "hit the blast"; being whipped around by the back wind of the engine propellers. I remember trying to be traditional and yell "Geronimo", but my short shallow breathing wouldn't allow it. Then just as suddenly, there was a total and eerie quiet. My T-10 parachute had deployed. I looked up and saw the beautiful 20' circle of nylon; my savior. I looked around and saw hundreds of parachutes as far as I could see in the night sky. I looked down and could see the white sand of the DZ highlighted by the black night. It was coming at me rapidly, and I was `absolutely powerless to stop my descent.

There was little time to soak in the beauty and excitement of the near-weightlessness during the float to ground. I had to unhook my GP and let it fall the full length of the 20 foot umbilical cord before I got too close to the ground. Then I had to prepare to land – do my PLF (parachute landing fall) to help absorb the full impact of hitting the ground. Toes pointed down, knees deeply bent, I fell backward slightly to my right, and allowed my boots and legs to roll over my shoulders.

And then, just like that, it was over. My 6th jump, my cherry jump. "Airborne, all the way!"

* * * * *

I had short periods of semi-sleep before the truck came to a final stop at the primary campsite. The driver jumped off, looked at me and pointed to his left. "Rio Chucunaque", he loudly and proudly proclaimed.

I jumped off the back of the truck with gleeful anticipation and followed the a few yards in the direction he was pointing. And there it was! FINALLY, I could see the soft powerful waters of the Chucunaque clearly reflected in the beaming headlights of the truck. I had reached the most important and obvious landmark by which to guide myself through the jungle. I would never be lost again.

Ha! I'm not much of a prophet.

How elated I was to have accomplished such a feat, and alone. My confidence soared. And I now knew I could make it to El Real – and be three fourths of the way to destination Colombia. I raised my fist and screamed out a jubilant "YES".

The driver politely introduced me to Alfredo, the camp's boss. He then proceeded to tell everyone the story of how they found me by the road; making vivid illustrations of how I was stalking around the night without any clothes on. He went on with hand gestures showing how fat my stomach had become after I'd eaten the whole loaf of bread. All of the camp's eight or ten people broke into an immediate laughter. Observing my laughter, the atmosphere quickly became warm and friendly; a feeling that remained during my entire stay at the camp. It was so good to be with people again.

This camp was larger than the previous camp I had visited. There were two gas lanterns and four oil lamps illuminating two large bamboo huts; one lamp hung by a nail on a large tree near the center of everything.

Alfredo expressed facial concerns about my health and quickly gave orders to have a hot meal for me and a place to sleep. He spoke broken English in a thick accent making it nearly impossible for us to communicate at first. In my broken Spanish with an equally thick accent we connected, and I somehow managed to explain why I was there. I added, that my hope was to catch a piraqua to El Real, hopefully tomorrow, and continue the journey into Colombia.

I threw that in just to impress him.

He displayed admiration for my courage (or was it stupidity?) and understood I was going to Colombia, but could not fully comprehend the real reason for such a dangerous journey. Alfredo added, there were very few canoes passing the campsite heading downstream for another month; near the end of the dry season. And, in a cautionary tone, he said the Chucunaque was dangerous and difficult to navigate in some parts.

I was greatly embarrassed when, after vividly describing my great hunger, I was unable to finish the medium sized portion of rice and fried fish prepared for me. My stomach had shrunken and was too stuffed with the undigested bread to receive more food.

A yawn reminded me and my hosts it was time for some sleep.

Alfredo led me to a bed in one of the camp's two standing buildings. It had thatched roofing and dormitory-style bamboo beds lined neatly in two rows; each fixed with a mosquito net hanging from a pole running across the ceiling. A thoughtful Alfredo retreated, allowing me to prepare a bed for the night.

It was another miserable night! The infected bites had become extremely sensitive to even the lightest touch of clothing.

The satisfaction of scratching had virtually disappeared. A new suffering came in the form of aching muscles. Each muscle, ligament, tendon and vein, everything under my skin, seemed to produce an aching pain. I tossed and turned, hoping for a satisfying angle, a good position, that would somehow ease the pain and relax my body; afford some peace of mind; and sooth my soul.

"My Soul"? I can't believe I was still thinking that!

Finally though, the dark dampness of the night dominated and I was able to duck under the veil of sleep; at least for a short while.

*   *   *   *   *

The inescapable sounds of men-in-motion forced me up, long before the sun had fully dissipated the fog from the surface of the Chucunaque River. Alfredo saw me stirring and cautioned me to hurry before the breakfast food got cold.

With a sigh, I raised myself and dropped my legs off the side of the bamboo bed and started the task of dressing and forcing the boots onto my swollen feet; a task becoming more and more difficult each day.

After eating as much rice as my shrunken stomach would allow, I sat back on the wooden bench to relax. And, for the first time, I took the opportunity to observe the campsite in daylight. The most obvious difference between this camp and the other were the two *women* busying themselves around the makeshift kitchen. One was an ageless old cook with a gleam in her eye and a grand toothless smile. The other was a young attractive woman; the wife of the truck driver who brought me to the camp last night.

The kitchen and the kitchen's fireplace occupied the center of the camp, around which all activities flowed. The fire was omnipresent, always burning. The two dormitory-like buildings were side by side between the fireplace and the river. Several small crude huts stood between the fireplace and the jungle containing greasy tools and other equipment. The camp was situated on top of the river bank surrounded by unusually tall, thin trees lacking the normal thick foliage of jungle growth. Soon the smell of coffee wisped through the air; giving the campsite a sense of security and a homelike feeling.

This relaxed mood directed my thoughts to self-care. I desperately needed a bath, and to avoid the possibility of embarrassment, retreated to a secluded spot by the river about a hundred yards downstream. Undressed, I edged my way into the water stepping through the soft brown mud. As I washed myself with the thin sliver of soap, I could see a score of small minnows nibbling at the scabs, infected areas, and blood spots from the recently picked ticks on my calves.

Drying in the cool air and warm sun, I took out the small flat mirror from the shaving kit and began an intense inspection of my face and body, especially those areas unable to be seen without the aid of a mirror.

I was shocked at what I saw: my face was gaunt and grey, wrinkles had formed around my sunken eyes and were filled with dirt, a tick clung to the skin just behind my earlobe, and for the first time I could see my hairline had receded. My hair was thinning and I was going bald. What a blow to the ego! I didn't want to believe I was looking older, but there it was. For the first time in my life I looked older than my actual age. I was twenty-six, but looked thirty-six or forty.

Ticks had found their way to the head of my penis, around my gonads, and at the crack of my anus. Laboriously, I picked and scraped until I could see no more; then I jumped back into the water for a second washing.

I was physically weakened and felt depressed as I dressed and returned to the camp. In a somber mood, I tested my patience by spending the remainder of the morning sitting on a log watching the uppermost bend in the river, hoping for a passing piraqua that might take me down the Chucunaque to El Real. But

I neither saw a boat nor heard the telling sounds of an outboard motor; none of which helped the depression. Delay increased my anxiety.

The inactivity of just sitting and waiting – although I badly needed the rest – had become intolerable. For nearly three weeks I had been in the Darien Jungle and on the move nearly all the time – going forward – toward the coveted goal of South America. I had to keep moving.

How to get to El Real? An unknown distance down river, I could walk; but my swollen and sore legs probably wouldn't get me far. I could swim – no, bad idea. I could build a raft and float down to El Real; there was plenty of balsa wood around the campsite. It would be great if I could fly – no, just a fantasy.

Patience, jackass, patience! I had to be patient for a while longer.

After lunch, one of the truck drivers and several of the workers told me I could travel with one of them to Santa Fe on a supply run. From there, they said, I could probably catch a ride to La Palma. Once there, they guessed it would be easy to ride a ferry boat to El Real; if the tide rose high enough.

There were just too many probable's, guesses, and "unknowns" to take them seriously. Plus, what was lost in translation. I really wasn't certain I understood what they were saying; there were too many unknowns. I remembered my admonition to myself earlier in the jungle to be wary of other people's opinion on knowledge of the Darien world. And this fed into my lack of trusting and need for self-reliance. All of my suspicions about human imperfections and frailties surfaced. So I discounted their advice.

I walked to the riverbank to be alone and to calm my emotions; I needed to cool off for a while. I didn't want to go around the damn jungle; I wanted to go *through* it. Plus, I didn't have any cash for a boat trip.

I'm hard-headed, and hate it when people try to tell me what to do. Especially when people want me to change my mind to fit their agenda – that stinks.

*   *   *   *   *

I had been patient long enough! It was again time to act!

With an abundance of balsa wood in the Darien Jungle I decided to build a raft! I would just float down the Chucunaque River to El Real; without the need of assistance from anyone.

I grabbed the machete and hurried into the surrounding trees near the campsite where it was easy to locate several tall balsa-looking trees. With all the energy of an angry crazy man I began hacking away, neatly dropping the tree in the pre-determined spot. After, marking off three equal sections of the long log, I sliced through each fifteen inch diameter of soft wood in less than an hour; then trimmed off all the branches.

I was possessed!

Dragging them separately to near the edge of the river, each of the three twelve foot pieces was neatly aligned on the ground. Next I scoured the area for yards and yards of thin pliable vines for tying them together. For added strength and safety, I cut and tied strong branches; maybe four inches in diameter, across both ends of what could then be called a raft. Like cross-arms, these two pieces were held in place by vines *and* wooden nails driven into the soft wood at opposite angles.

Making the raft complete, I built a small rack, or stand, on the center log near what I considered the front. This could be a place on which to tie the sleeping gear and saddle bags, and would be high enough to keep my boots away from the water that would seep in between the logs.

Eventually I found a long narrow tree to cut and trim for use as a steering and pushing pole to guide the raft downstream. The pole was long, sturdy, and straight, yet slender enough to fit the grip of my hands.

I was ready to launch.

With much hoopla from several loggers, I pushed the raft into the water tethered by a vine. It slowly floated downstream several yards from the muddy riverbank, and appeared in good order. Then, in what seemed like an hour – but was probably only a few minutes - the raft sunk under the surface of the water in a slow bubbly fizzle. It didn't sink to the bottom or out of sight. It just floated under the water at about six or eight inches of depth.

I was crushed and bewildered and could only stand there in stunned disbelief staring at the spot where once was my proud creation, unable to distinguish between the need to laugh or cry. The growing number of onlookers began to laugh and whistle, pointing to the spot in the river where the craft was hovering under water; this added to my indignation.

But Alfredo quickly sensed the predicament of the situation and quietly took charge, ordering several of the men to assist me with building another raft.

The men, three of them, chose a different looking balsa tree to cut down; actually cutting down *two* of them. Cutting each tree into three sections, we dragged each section to the water's edge and gathered a bundle of tying vines. After lashing the first three logs together, the remaining three logs were placed *on top* of the first three and tied down crisscrossed with the under logs. A sturdy rack was constructed and tied to what became the front of the raft.

Within half the time it took me to build the first one, and twice the size, the loggers had expertly completed an inspiring raft. This one, thanks to their expertise, floated very well. It also held my weight and gear perfectly.

With the raft ready to go and the day almost gone, I thanked Alfredo and the men; I boasted that I would be leaving early in the morning for El Real.

*   *   *   *   *

Why is it so hard for me to ask for help? To ask for advice? I could have saved a lot of time and energy with

building the raft if I would have just asked. Maybe I should take their advice and get to El Real another way?

*   *   *   *   *

After dinner, Alfredo drew me into a conversation in hopes of learning more English, and at the same time trying to help me. He had watched my raft-building efforts with the eye of a critic who was about to pass judgment; but he didn't. He just moved graciously about, speaking of many things and places. Alfredo was a paradox. At six feet two inches tall he was a giant of a man; weighing over two hundred and fifty pounds, but with the physical dexterity of an athlete. His face sported a heavy black beard, and at first sight looked more like a slow learner than the engineer he actually was. But you quickly knew he had a mind as sharp as a whip.

The pleasing tone of his voice rarely altered, except maybe when directed toward the nasty insects. He was poetic as he talked of a brother working in a quiet, clean office in Panama City, while he, with an equal amount of education, worked in the jungle simply because he did not learn to speak good English.

He thought the relationship between United States and Latin America was now much better than in the past, but wanted to know: "Why American touristos no speakie's Spanish?" and "Why have they so much *dineros*?" These were good questions but they made me somewhat defensive.

Before the sun had set fully, Alfredo proceeded politely to out-debate me on almost every subject we talked about. Although he thought I was doing the wrong thing by traveling in the jungle alone, and expressed the dangers of rafting down the Chucunaque River, he had offered to do everything within his powers to help. He was a man I admired.

*   *   *   *   *

Insomnia-filled nights with short periods of light sleep had become the norm for me; this night was no exception. It seemed as if the infected bites always began to complain when it was time to sleep. Perhaps it was the inactivity at night and the adrenalin during the day. No matter. By morning my feet and calves had swollen so badly that only the lack of medical supplies in the camp prevented me from staying.

I tried to force on the boots but decided to tie them to the rack on the raft. Even sitting on the wooden bench at the breakfast table caused the blood to rush to my lower extremities causing my ankles and each toe to pound with pain; it was as though they were ready to explode.

But I had to leave.

They were all there to see me go, the whole camp. The old cook presented me with a small bag of food; Alfredo slipped me an unopened pack of cigarettes; the toothless truck-driver smiled glowingly. All of them gave a cautious but cheerful goodbye. Repeatedly, I thanked them for their life-saving help and warm hospitality.

Pants rolled to the knees, gear tied to the rack, pole in hand, I cast off from the shore and was on my way down the river to El Real in a flash.

Chapter 7

The slow current carried me away from the camp and down the muddy Chucunaque River on the bobbing raft of balsa wood. A quick glance back and I saw the group of brotherly Panamanian loggers and their two women huddled on the edge of the riverbank staring in silence. An overhanging tree branch began to block my view as I rounded the first bend, and they were out of sight. Once again I was alone and on my own.

A slight twinge of remorse crept over me. For an instant I wanted to rush back and say *"Muchas gracias."* again; say goodbye again. I wanted to tell them I would one day return to Panama to see them, but I knew it would never happen.

Looking downstream, the morning sun was rising to the tree tops and the glassy water reflected its brightness into my eyes, curing me of the melancholy and restoring my awareness to the immediate problem of rafting this craft down the uncertain river.

* * * * *

The eccentric body of the Darien environment had radically changed again, posing yet another danger. The new face was liquid water and the danger lay in its ever-changing look – alternating between wide and narrow, fast and slow, smooth and rough, jagged rocks and piles of broken branches.

I would often be floating smoothly along the quiet riverbanks when suddenly, like the prolonged rolling of distant thunder getting closer, I could feel the destructive pounding of water rushing against the many stationary boulders. Hanging on for dear life, I could only feel the raft being thrown down the convulsive rapids slung by the untamable current.

The guiding pole so exquisitely chosen, cut and trimmed at the campsite was no match for the strength of the onrushing current and could not withstand the oppressive tons of water. It broke once, twice, then three times until only a yard-long stub remained. Without steerage, the raft was forced to obey the natural currents; causing it to carom from rock to rock.

I was out of control! (Nothing unusual about that.)

My clothing stayed wet from the constant water splash hitting me from every direction. My bare feet, gripping the bark of the balsa logs on the swaying raft, seemed to be under water more often than not. Wet and stringy hair pasted my scalp and hung over my eyes to obstruct my vision. It took all my strength to hold onto the peeling balsa logs; I hoped that the soft banks of the mighty Chucunaque would soon thwart the charging waters and swallow the rushing rapids before it swallowed me; a mere speck in a grand universe.

Then, inevitably as a storm ends, tranquility returned. The pounding rush of water subsided, and the river became peaceful and quiet. With a sigh of relief, I could stand upright and move about the raft to check the equipment and tug the vines holding the craft together. The nightmarish memory remained, but it was as though it had never happened. Once again I heard the musical voices of distant birds and smelled the passing fragrance of sweet flowers.

The river became smooth and wide and the raft floated listlessly along. The light brown water quietly lapped over an occasional surface rock, while I enjoyed the warm rays of the drying sun. Sometimes it was difficult to detect any forward motion; it was as if there was no movement.

But the placidness of the backwaters only added to my laboring frustrations. Without a long pole or rudder, steering was impossible. As the raft floundered about the slow motion whirlpools, following the whim of each little current or cross-current, it would make slow three-hundred and sixty degree turns, and sometimes appeared to be going upstream. Several times I jumped into the water attempting to swim and paddle the raft from behind, pushing it out of the squandering backwater.

Even the peace of the quiet backwaters, however, was no protection from the unforgiving jungle. Overhanging branches completely shredded what remained of the sweat-stained shirt, and etched long scratches down my back and arms.

It was a never ending obstacle course.

I probably could have opted to swim and tow the raft to one of the riverbanks to seek another pole, but by the time I could see an opening large enough in the continuous stretch of outcropped trees along either side to land the craft, it was too late; the current carried the raft past. And secretly, I liked the forward motion; I was getting closer to El Real.

Once the raft bumped into a high uneven pile of logs and branches, and I was able to pull out a long dried pole; it was thicker than the original, shorter than hoped for, but good enough. I smoothed it off with the machete, moved the raft away from the pile, and regained some degree of control of direction,

The Chucunaque carried me down its pathway under suspended logs, the spinning backwaters, past huge boulders, and through narrow channels – a deluge of forgotten life.

Again I am shattered. Would I never learn? What a terrible idea to think I could build a raft, for I knew nothing of raft-building; float it down the Chucunaque, for I knew nothing

of the Chucunaque; and have a nice and pleasant ride to El Real, for I knew nothing of the distance to El Real. What was it: arrogance, pride, hard-headedness, or just plain stupidity?

Only then did I recall the conversation with Alfredo as he tried to coach me of the dangers of the Rio Chucunaque. Why hadn't I heeded his warnings? Why wouldn't I heed anybody's warnings? If I didn't soon learn to accept the knowledge and wisdom of others, I would surely die.

*   *   *   *   *

The raft floated past one tributary of the Chucunaque whose waters came from the north – to my left – and shortly thereafter became wedged in a log-jam; its forward progress stopped abruptly. It was solidly stuck between two large boulders by a multitude of logs, branches, twigs, and vines. It would not move.

Suddenly disenchanted with the idea of floating down river to El Real, I momentarily entertained the idea of abandoning the raft to try walking the riverbanks. This way, my movements would be more constant and I would be more in control.

But I had no idea where my position on the map was. Nobody from the campsite knew their exact location on the Chucunaque River. They only knew I was *somewhere* on the Chucunaque. And, judging by the slow drifting pace so far, it would probably take many days to get to El Real. Stuck again!

The tributary could have been any one of a dozen coming down from the mountain range bordering the Atlantic side of the Darien isthmus, so I decided to stay with the raft for at least another twenty-four hours and hope for the best.

After a solid hour of hacking away at the wooden debris jamming the passageway, the raft squeezed through the temporary opening. The force of the current freed the raft; swiftly moving it downstream. Free once again.

The raft picked up speed. Soon the steady roaring sounds of rapids reached my ears. My adrenalin level bumped up. I *knew* *the* rapids were not far away. I feared the worst, as the raft rounded a bend and continued to gain speed. By this time, the raft was bobbing like a cork on top of churning white water. My body felt the deafening noise, as I struggled to maintain stability of the jerking raft.

I stretched my neck looking down over the cascading water, but could see neither an end of the moss-capped rocks nor a smooth passageway through which to guide the beamy raft.

A sudden fear ran through my body as I realized I had to raft down the largest, most dangerous rapids I had ever seen. Desperately, I tried to maneuver the craft to the riverbank, but to no avail. As before, the pole broke into several smaller pieces. It was quickly obvious that any attempt to steer the raft in any direction was impossible.

I fell down onto the moistened logs of balsa, with one arm hanging on the rack and the other around one of the logs, hoping the raft would somehow finds its way through. Intuition, however, told me my rafting adventures were nearing an end.

A sudden jolt caused by the raft scraping over several large rocks just above the water level rocked my body. But the powerful force of the onrushing current kept the raft moving further downriver.

Again, I felt the jar from the raft banging against a series of rocks. This time I slid backward near the back of the tied balsa as the raft's logs somehow became wedged on several rounded rocks, and I was pushing it deeper into the water.

For a brief, time the raft was stationary. Then the relentless current slowly moved the rear of the craft under the water, and I thought it was time to go down with the ship. Desperately holding on, I tried to preserve the still dry equipment. I couldn't think of what to do next.

As the end of the raft sunk deeper and deeper under the surface of the water, the current slowly pushed the sunken end of the raft downriver, pulling it off the slippery rock and slinging us down the rapids like a shot from a sling.

The raft moved across the top of the bubbling water so fast it was impossible to clearly distinguish features of the surrounding jungle. There was only the white water below and blue sky above; everything else was just a blur.

The excessive speed came to a sudden stop for the last time when the raft made a crash landing on several boulders, causing me to roll to the back of the raft (which was actually the front), and nearly into the water. Luckily, the equipment rack stopped me as I desperately clutched onto the saddle-bags and sleeping roll.

At that instant, the onrushing water came over the logs and washed me off the raft and into the cold rapids with a great shock. Out the corner of my eye, I saw my boots still dangling from the rack.

Frantically I began splashing my way toward the closest green of the jungle, as the rapids twisted and banged my body against the rocks. Dizzied by the swirling rapids and punishing rocks, I was not sure of my direction. Water rushed up my nose and filled my eyes, and I was coughing water out of my lungs.

Even as the water became chest-deep, I was forced into some semblance of swimming due to the power of the current. Occasionally I could bounce off the bottom toward more shallow water while holding the equipment high; as the current carried me farther downriver.

I was able to push myself in front of a huge boulder and regain a sense of balance and direction. I stayed in its hallowed protection and moved higher into knee deep water. Then, with saddle-bags held high and sleeping gear under arm, I scrambled to the dry rocky banks on my hands and knees and flopped into some tall grass, choking and vomiting, but thankful to be alive.

As my sense of equilibrium returned, survival, always a first thought, flashed through my mind as I made a quick check of the drenched equipment for the bare essentials. The machete, tied to the sleeping roll, was there. The saddle-bags had been strapped closed, and my passport and money inside remained dry in a plastic bag.

Feeling secure and looking down at my throbbing ankles and white wrinkled toes, I suddenly remembered my boots. They were still on the raft! I knew I would never be able to travel even one mile in the jungle terrain without them.

I would have to go back into the water to retrieve them off the raft.

Feeling half confident, half uncertain, I lightly jogged up the rock-studded river bank about two hundred yards until I was at its shortest distance from the shore. The boots were still there, tied and dangling from the raft, which was still stuck on the rocks.

I continued upriver for another difficult two hundred yards from where the raft was located and recklessly dove into the water to begin the struggle back to the raft.

Without the burden of the equipment, I was surprised at the ease with which I was able to reach the spot where the raft was perched. Edging my way toward the boots, the tied six logs of the raft were separating under the pressure of the current. I saw the boots tied to the rack floating downstream, not five yards away. The rack momentarily got stuck on a protruding branch, and, with the little energy I had left, I swam and splashed my way until the current floated me directly in line with my boots.

With both hands I grasped at the strings and held them tightly as the current continued to push me downriver. Clutching the strings in my left fist, I began the grueling task of getting myself back to shore.

I was exhausted and short of breath. The water-soaked boots restricted me to the use of one arm for swimming and staying above water. The curling waves repeatedly forced me under water. Seized by fear, I wanted to abandon the boots, but knew if I did, death was inevitable.

I wanted to live! But I didn't have the physical strength to withstand the forces of nature. For the first time in my life I admitted I *wanted* to live.

As the river came to a bend, I started pushing myself off the bottom of the riverbed toward the shoreline until I reached a quiet pool of water where I energized long enough to move closer to shore. Rock by rock I crawled on my stomach and hands and knees until I was lying in only a few inches of water and mud. Physically beaten, exhausted, and gasping for air, I lunged forward onto terra firma clutching the boots and happy to be alive.

*   *   *   *   *

What happened after I reached the safety of the river bank and the jungle trees became hazy in my mind – possibly losing consciousness? I do remember having a brief flashback on a previous water trauma.

*   *   *   *   *

The deafening wind howled across the top of the high ocean waves as drops of rain struck the skin on my face like hot pellets from a shotgun. Called out of semi-sleep from a warm bunk by the captain, I was ordered on deck. The hatch on the starboard pontoon was taking water and he wanted me to caulk it closed. His close friend, Larry Krebs, would help.

The captain was – at least to us – the fabled Fenton J. Kilkinney, the master of many sailing ships to most of the ports in and around the Pacific and Indian Oceans. This boat was the "Sea Gypsy"; a 30' trimaran built by four of us paratroopers on Okinawa with the help of a few local boat-builders. The four of us – Bill (Hinkle, again), Brad, Doug, and I – were short on sailing experience but long on chutspa. We tied the time of the completion of the boat building efforts to our discharge from the military – early in September, 1961. Three of us worked at Headquarters of the 2nd/503rd and were able to finagle our discharge from the military on Okinawa. At the same time, we scrounged most of our food supplies, medical supplies, and a small radio off the military. We used alcohol to ply Kilkinney into being our captain. Our plan was to sail out of Buckner Bay in high hope of eventually sailing across the Pacific via the Southern route back home to America.

Larry Krebs was the owner and editor of the only English-speaking magazine on Okinawa, and wanted to sail with us to the Philippine Islands with the idea of writing a story about it. Everyone agreed to bring him along, even though six on a 30' sailboat would be burdensome; and it was our shakedown cruise.

The Sea Gypsy sailed from Okinawa on December 1, 1961; headed due south.

Nearly half way to the Philippines we were hit by a powerful typhoon. The wind and waves grew stronger and higher with each passing hour. Captain Kilkenny could feel the boat listing to starboard, and knew the sliding hatch was taking water because it was repeatedly being forced under water.

Larry, being a lot older than my twenty-two years, led the project. He insisted I have a line of rope tied around my waist and had it lashed to the mast. I slowly crept onto the pontoon, caulking tube in my hand. The pitching, rocking, and rolling of the boat made the job of caulking extremely difficult. But finally, I finished it.

Crawling on hands and knees back to the mast at amidships, I started to untie myself as Larry began untying the line from his end. At that moment in time, the Sea Gypsy took a humongous wave from the starboard side, washing Larry overboard on the port side. Ironically, I too would have been thrown overboard had Larry not insisted I be lashed to the mast.

It was one of those moments when time stands still; it remains seared in my memory forever. I reached down toward the water from the port pontoon vainly trying to reach him. At the same time, he reached up from the water, grasping, hoping to catch my hand or anything.

Our eyes met. For the briefest of moments we were locked together for an eternity – eyeball to eyeball. I saw the whites of his pleading eyes. We both knew he was a dead man.

It has become a scene relived in my mind over and over nearly every day.

I ran to the stern, pushed by the typhoon winds, yelling at the top of my lungs: "MAN OVERBOARD! MAN OVERBOARD! MAN OVERBOARD!" Reaching the captain on the tiller, I simultaneously grabbed the round life preserver off the back of the cabin roof and threw it with all my might as long and hard as I could toward Larry. But already he was just a tiny spot bobbing from the top to the trough of the waves.

Everyone was on deck by now, stretching our bodies. We saw him swim to the white round corked life preserver, and slip it over his head. But that was the last we, or anyone, every saw of Larry Krebs.

Captain Kilkinney brought the trimaran about, of course. But a boat like that had a very wide beam, with three hulls broadside against the wind, making it very difficult to bring about; many times more difficult in voracious typhoon conditions. We made numerous crossing patterns, but resigned that only luck would bring us together.

Kilkinney sent out a continuous stream of SOS's, and by daylight a Chinese merchant ship reached us to relay the emergency information to Okinawa. We sailed the Sea Gypsy westerly to the nearest Japanese island, Ishigaki, and hovered in the safety of the island's harbor until the storm passed.

An air-sea rescue operation was conducted by the military, but to no avail. It was called off by December 9th. We were all interviewed, separately and collectively, by the proper authorities. His mother came. It was all very sad. Larry was an intelligent and fun-loving guy, as well as an important person in the region. We all had a kinship with him.

Ironic as it may be, this was the <u>second</u> time Larry had been washed overboard and was lost at sea. Obviously, he had been found and rescued the first time.

The collective dream ended, and we separated ways. I never saw Captain Kilkenny again; nor Doug. Bill and I continued on; we flew back to Okinawa, then back to the States. Our friendship endured the test of time. I visited Brad once, in Butte (or Billings) Montana while driving cross-country from Pennsylvania to California with my good friend Jack McKinney who did most of the driving. We got a little drunk and reminisced.

They still used silver dollars in that bar...

$$*\quad*\quad*\quad*\quad*$$

I lay on the riverbank, half dry, half wet, in and out of consciousness. When I finally came out of the states of multi-awareness, I wrote the following journal notes:

March 6, 1965 –

How long had I lain here in the muck and mire? Who knows? Who cares?

Time does not matter. One side of me said "This is cool." The other side thought it was stupid. Here I am lying by a nearly unknown river in an infamous jungle...Why? Fate, the blameful one, is always playing tricks on me. My soul, by any other name...had been battered, stretched, until it had been pricked with a hole – but that was probably long ago. Is this how to fill it – with everything coming in from the outside? Nah! If my soul is inside, it must be an "inside job". There are natural laws, but what the hell are they? I'm beginning to think I can survive <u>anything</u>. The jungle and I were one. Something within was indestructible; would live forever. What? I didn't know. I know I will make it through the god-forsaken jungle to South America, and back to the states. Even if...I had to do it on my hands and knees. The longing was over.

*   *   *   *   *

"Ha", I said with a smile, "if only the folks back home could see me now." The grin remained on my face as I began to concentrate on the immediacy and gravity of the situation at hand. Two logs of the raft stuck upright in the rapids against some rocks, forming a "V"; a victory of nature over ideals; or was it wishful thinking? The shakedown cruise was perilously close to being over.

Sitting there, I dumped the water from the saddle-bags, spread my jacket on the sand and rocks to dry, and threw what was left of my shredded jungle-rotted stockings in the river. The two cans of C-rations were still there to start me thinking about food and eating. A long string of items had been strewn along my path from the beginning to lighten the carrying load, but I was now down to a few precious possessions. The only things not necessary were two empty C-ration cans, and a few extra feet of rope. I threw these items into the dense jungle foliage. And, even though rendered useless from the wetness, I decided to keep the handful of twenty-two bullets.

In the dusk, it was easy to know darkness was less than an hour away. Another incredible day was about to end. "Where to sleep" was no longer a novelty to excite me. I just wanted two trees close enough together to string the hammock and stretch the mosquito net, and get off my feet to relieve the pounding rush of blood in my lower extremities.

The monotonous pouring rapids provided some solace, allowing me a few hours of sleep.

*   *   *   *   *

In the morning I walked to the river's edge to wash. The indentations in the mud from my standing body were already several inches deep when I heard an unusual sound. Just the sound of some logs against the rocks in the rapids, I thought.

Fortunately it was another familiar sound. Suddenly, a long piraqua came shooting down the rapids with flat sprays of water breaking over its bow. In it was three Panamanians, and the boat was filled with camping equipment.

Springing to my tender feet, I began yelling for their attention. They must have had prior warning – probably by the men at the logging camp – because the piraqua pointed straight for the riverbank without hesitation and came to rest in the soft mud just a few feet from me.

Two of the three men quickly jumped onto the riverbank; loaded me and my equipment aboard, pushed the canoe back into the moving water, and headed downstream without saying one word. A short thin man with a well-used hat gave me a lit cigarette as we motored to the middle and used the currents of the Chucunaque to speed us along.

Inexplicably, the worst of the rapids were behind us.

*   *   *   *   *

After the initial shock of being rescued wore off, and I was able to catch my breath, I became brave enough to use my sloppy Spanish and ask where we were going. "Yaviza" was their answer, and we would be there by late tomorrow.

Again I had been saved from the hazards of the jungle by the activities of other humans. I wanted to laugh and cry at the same time – safe until Yaviza. Yaviza was the sister-city of El Real. Once there I would be three-quarters of the way through the jungle to Colombia.

No more worries of food, no more worries about water, and no more worries about walking on swollen feet for at least two days. I was so elated. There was glowing warmth welling inside me for all the human compassion and companionship bestowed upon me.

The three, all Negros, not only saved my life, but were also transporting me to *somewhere*; to some sort of civilization.

I had done it! With the help of others, I had made it! I could not die now. Tomorrow, or very soon, food, medicine, clothing would be forthcoming.

The following day I would hobble triumphantly into Yaviza and El Real.

Nothing could stop me now.

Chapter 8

I never fully understood why the three men were traveling the
Chucunaque, or what they were doing so far back in the
interior of the jungle. The equipment on board was mostly
covered with a small tarp, and I was unable to identify the little
that was visible. I suspected they were prospecting for gold. But
their skill at maneuvering the piraqua through the rapids and
other obstacles was impressive. Stopping often for rest, food, and
forays into the jungle with their twenty-two rifles (I had given
them my few remaining bullets), it was an easy-going and
nonchalant trip.

By evening, the elder of the three proudly stated we
would have a place to sleep within thirty minutes, adding
credence to their knowledge of the river. Their differences in age
– one a stately elder, one a quiet middle-aged responsible type,
and the other young and full of energy - made up the classic
family of three generation males, although they were very
different in appearance.

As foretold, the canoe skidded to a stop on a muddy bank
next to an acre of land made glaringly obvious by the absence of
trees and shrubbery. It was the largest single clearing I'd seen

since entering Darien Jungle; it was probably the site of an old abandoned logging camp.

After unloading a few supplies and lifting me onto the grass, the four of us stood near the center of the circled clearing. Even in my weakened condition I was over-awed by the spectacle of the campsite: there were three thoroughly rusted-out World War II *cannons* sitting just to the left; to the right were four old and dilapidated US Army *trucks* of the half-ton size. What they were doing there or how they came to rest there was beyond the powers of my wildest imagination. Added to the hoary spectacle, a huge pile of rotten and decayed logs, nearly thirty feet high, was strewn together behind the long shack at the far end of the circle. The sun set caste a golden glow over the jungle clearing to further enhance the bizarre sight.

In the dimming light, a bearded middle-aged man came out of the lonely shack to greet us. A handshake and a smile between them indicated they were friends and had experienced other meetings.

The elder from the canoe introduced this Robinson Crusoe-type as the watchman of the camp. He was a strange hermit-looking type. I thought it must be the loneliest job in the world; sitting in the middle of nowhere, guarding nothing.

After the men from the canoe told him of how they found me (and probably added the information from Alfredo at the logging camp), he let out a long high pitched whistle and shook his head in disbelief. Questioning, he repeated "Panama City?" several times, shook my hand, and gave me a long flinching look.

The uneasiness was soon forgotten when, after helping to tie my hammock between two poles in the shack, he and the others set about preparing the evening meal. Each man seemed to know exactly what he was to do, as if they had done this a hundred times before. A bursting fire quickly brought a blackened pot of water to a boil, which soon became a stew. It consisted of jungle potatoes, wild-rice, fried bananas, and a recently killed fowl that looked like a dark-feathered turkey, only smaller.

The constant pain deterred thoughts of food until the rich smell of stew reached my nostrils. When the food was placed before me I ate with relish, as if it were my last meal. The hot stew burned my tongue after the first spoonful, but the warm glowing sensation in my stomach was satisfaction enough, even though fire ashes and moths were clearly visible floating on top.

After the last bit of stew was spooned from the pot and eaten, we five sat around the fire drinking stale coffee and dabbling in simple conversation, interrupted occasionally by a few hand slaps against our bare skin hoping to kill a biting mosquito. I wanted to learn more about this watchman who displayed a certain tranquility toward everything and everybody. But pain and weariness prevented any in-depth exchanges between us; the three from the canoe directed their movements toward sleep.

Once in the hammock, I tried to bury myself in thoughts of Yaviza, El Real, Colombia and the future, but concentration became impossible. The pain, itching, and especially the mosquitoes caused me a torturous feeling of disconnectedness from myself and the world, and would not allow that sleep, the sleep of Macbeth:

> *"Me thought I heard a voice cry 'Sleep no more*
> *Macbeth does murder sleep," the innocent sleep,*
>
> *sleep that knits up the ravell'd sleave of care,*
> *The death of each day's life, sore labour's bath,*
>
> *Balm of hurt minds, great nature's second course,*
> *Chief nourisher in life's feast... "*

I was forced to memorize that in school, but the old Bard knew what he was talking about.

I prayed for daylight, but it did not come. The long night, a universal timepiece, wore on as the earth revolved around the sun, and the sun held by gravity in a galaxy, speeding through space. I wondered if there was a center of creation; of time and space; of the agonies and ecstasies. I did not sleep a wink the entire night.

*   *   *   *   *

Before fully realizing it, the shack and campsite were beginning to have form and color. Triumphantly, the dawn had at last begun! The watchman was the first of the Panamanians to stir. He momentarily hovered nearby, and our crust-laden eyes connected through the sheer mosquito net as if he had been aware of my nocturnal ordeal. The light of the new dawn deflected our eyes toward the doorway greeting the new day. With a soft laugh and a quiet statement to himself, he walked to the opposite end of the hut to wake the others. The three river-men arose without hesitation and began buzzing around the campsite fire with great enthusiasm, anticipating the sun's rising.

Crawling around the earthen floor like an animal, I rolled up the sleeping gear and buckled the saddle bags in preparation for the boat ride to Yaviza. I really wasn't very hungry, having just eaten eight hours previously. The need for medicine, something, to heal the infectious bites preoccupied my consciousness. Pain relief motivated my every decision.

A breakfast of dried fish, fried bananas, and some well-cooked rice stimulated everyone for departure. One of the men carried my gear while the other two helped me to the river and into the piraqua. A sincere handshake with the watchman, an effortless castoff, and the canoe was headed to the middle of the river as the blazing sun sprinkled welcomed rays through the forest jungle trees.

At first the engine, chilled by the long damp night, refused to start. The helmsman pulled and pulled the rope without letup until finally, in a cloud of blue-grey smoke, it started. Rattling at first, the engine settled into a smooth rhythm and the piraqua moved downstream at a brisk five or six miles per hour.

*   *   *   *   *

About mid-afternoon, the helmsman brought the canoe to a stop by a small patch of flat green grass for a rest and a quick meal of fried bananas and leftover rice wrapped in a banana leaf. I remained in the boat during the meal for fear of antagonizing the leg infections. Some of the swelling had marginally subsided.

Again underway, the big question became: "When will we be in Yaviza?" It was a question repeated about once per hour. As the late afternoon turned into early evening, it became increasingly obvious arrival in Yaviza would not be until after dark.

Nonetheless I could feel the excitement growing with each mile of traveled river water. More and more frequently the banks of the Chucunaque were spotted with thatched-roofs and Indian activity. At first, only a few huts were scattered about every two or three miles apart, separating themselves from the jungle thicket. Then, every quarter-mile, Panamanian frontiersmen dotted the shoreline until each house or hut was nearly within sight and sound of each other, like the gradual cluttering of billboards forecasting the entrance into a city.

As dusk turned to darkness, the river way was lighted by the jagged reflections of burning torches from both sides of the river, illuminating our faces. Then the quiet middle-aged man sitting on the bow of the canoe turned his head toward us and proudly stated "Mi Casa." – home – was just ahead.

Before us, like neat patterns of hundreds of fireflies, was my first sign of real civilization in exactly three weeks. It was the night of March seventh. Black and shapeless, the outline of Yaviza filled me with the first *real* glimmer of hope since the beginning, before the ravages of the jungle took its toll. The thirst, the starvation, the pain and even the infected bug bites now seemed worthwhile.

After all, an easy river trail to the Colombian border, and it was over. I wanted to jump for joy and shout *hallelujah*; shake hands with everyone. Instead, I sat quietly, almost sheepishly, in the canoe until it came to a complete stop by the low wooden docks at Yaviza.

*   *   *   *   *

*It's hard for me to accept, but a person can now comfortably **drive** a car, truck, motorcycle, or anything from Panama city to Yaviza.*

*   *   *   *   *

I didn't know what to expect. There was nobody there, not one person, as the piraqua slid slowly through the dark greasy waters beneath a fifty-foot earthen cliff and bounced to a halt.

Most of the villagers lived in huts on the flat ground twenty five feet above the river's water level; a hundred in all. Still the night was devoid of sounds, except for the low mumbling of our own voices and the faint barking of a distant dog.

Prudently the three men unloaded their belongings, carrying bundles up the clay stairs to the top of the cliff. Soon spirited female voices could be heard greeting their homecoming husbands; they too helped with the unloading. They then unloaded and carried *me* to the top and to the home of the eldest of the three. It was an unusual sight to see that every house, shack, or hut within sight was built on stilts holding their living quarters at least four feet above the ground.

But it was getting late, and I was quickly helped into the house and placed in a hammock, surrounded by seven small children and several adults staring intently. Strange, but I could not remember sleeping inside the home of a Negro. They lived no differently, but the reversal of circumstances caught me by surprise. Although I had spent time in the Japanese culture, this was the first time I actually had the experience of feeling what it was like being a minority.

Their eyes seemed sympathetic toward my chalk-white skin, unruly hair, the dirt, the grime, and festered ankles. They must have thought of me as inferior. Not because of race, but because it was obvious I didn't know the jungle, could not speak Spanish, and was medically in need. In their eyes, I was either crazy, dumb, or both.

Their humanity surfaced. In less than thirty minutes, I was presented with a bowl of steamed rice, dried fish, and hot coffee. And, almost as if they read my mind, they moved me from the hammock to a more comfortable looking cot prepared with two thin, clean, blankets and a small pillow. Finally, I had a pillow to rest my weary head. Medical aid would have to wait until morning, as I flopped on the cot too exhausted to undress, converse, or think.

Despite the caffeine, it was my best night's sleep in the Darien; no dreams; no insomnia; no itching attacks; just a pure blissful sleep.

*   *   *   *   *

In the morning, I noted someone had undressed and tucked me under the covers during the silence of the night. And before I was fully cognizant, I was greeted with the sight of two men in green uniforms standing nearby. It was the Panamanian Military National Guard wanting me to go to the Police Station to check my credentials.

Not a word was spoken as I raised my sore and stiff body from the canvas cot, dressed and wobbled my way to the door. Dizzy and weakened, I turned around at the doorway and said: "Gracias para todo." several times to the entire watching household, wondering if I would ever see them again.

The swelling had decreased and the throbbing pain was less intense as the two guards carried my equipment and I tip-toed onto the streets of Yaviza; boots slung over my shoulders. It was early morning and most of the town's children, playing in the earthen streets, saw me and began running around us, pointing fingers, and laughing; one even reached out and touched me. Other than the children and a few political posters haphazardly hanging on trees, I didn't get to see much of the surrounding village. I did get to see the spot where the Chucunaque and another un-named river merged. The policemen barked a few harmless orders at the children causing them to temporarily scatter, but they soon returned to the spectacle at hand.

Once inside the station, the policemen seemed as amused with me as I was with them. But they were extremely helpful. Rummaging through what little gear I had left, they quickly okayed my credentials. They only asked about firearms. Fortunately I didn't have a weapon (otherwise it would have meant several weeks of delay to verify) and I had given away the

Approximate Route from Panama City
Through the Darien Jungle
To Turbo, Colombia

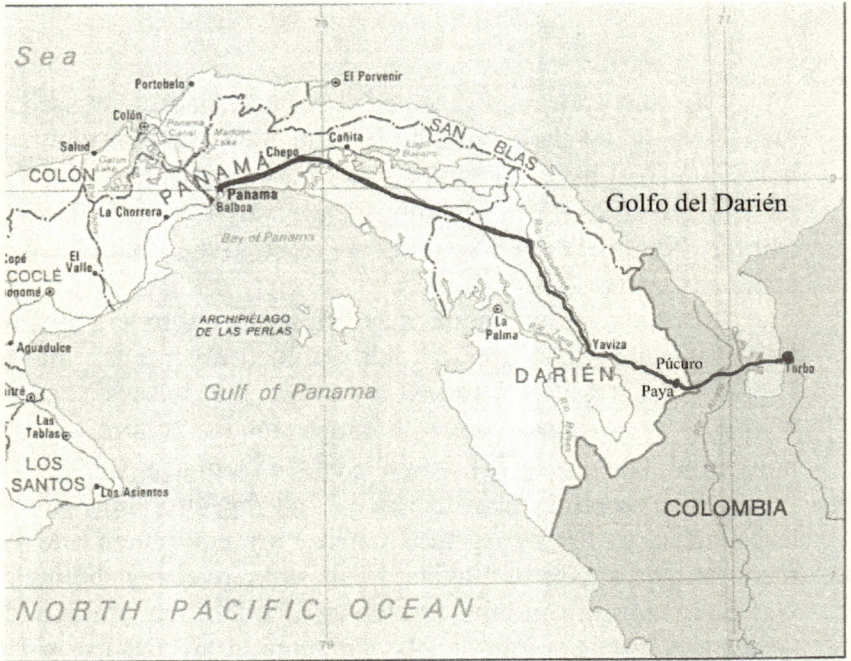

Base B02395 (540285) 5-95

last of the twenty-two bullets.

Knowing I was weaponless, they were even *more* willing to help; they permitted use of their barrel of rain-water for bathing and shaving, donating food and cigarettes, and even appointing a personal guard to show me the village.

With nothing left of my last shirt and without stockings, the guard led me to one of only *two* general stores in Yaviza. Clad only in dungarees, the guard was forced to "strongly convince" the Chinese owner of the store to cash two of my ten dollar traveler's checks.

Cash in hand, I bought two shirts, several pair of stockings, and some cans of food. Dark chocolate stains on my fingers and a bottle of soda pop in hand, I bought a container of antibiotic pills and some very good ointment for my legs; swallowing pills and rubbing ointment while browsing through the isles. Already I was feeling better, if only psychologically.

Once back in the Police Station, I experienced the only uncomfortable event while in Yaviza. Knowing I was an American, the Police summoned two young missionaries living in the Yaviza-El Real area, Johnny and Alec. Starved for conversation, I rapidly shared my story and of the sometimes wonderful and sometimes frightening experiences thus far. Their almost apathetic reaction and impatient body language took me aback.

Instead of furthering this conversation, they began telling me a story about Jesus Christ being the Son of God and the Savior of the universe, and of all the good they were doing by "saving the savages" of the Darien Jungle from the devil. They asked if I was a religious person, and of which faith.

I responded, while not an atheist, I had no preference for an organized religion and was most likely categorized a questioning agnostic. They jerked up in unison, nearly coming out of their seats, to say they would "wrestle into me" the faith of Jesus if they could. I did my diplomatic best to change the topic of conversation and prevent anyone embarrassment; yet they persisted.

Finally, I bluntly said I was not in the Darien Jungle looking to be saved, but merely wanting conversation – not *conversion* – and didn't want to be lectured about something I considered very personal. With this, Johnny and Alec politely broke off the conversation, softly shook my hand and said goodbye. I never saw them again.

They were young men of my own age, healthy looking and well-groomed. Because of our contrasting situations, perhaps my expectations were too high. I secretly was hoping for a meal at the missionary because, on a human level, we were just 3 American guys in a foreign country thrown together by circumstances. Instead the two climbed onto a powered canoe, crossed to the opposite bank of the Chucunaque, and returned to their private mission. The only bit of advice they offered was the uselessness of going to El Real because it was five miles out of my way. I had a slight inkling they may have been homosexuals; but nothing factual on which to base it. It was not important, but just a feeling.

What are these queers doing here in the middle of the jungle anyway? They should be trying to convert <u>themselves</u>, rather than me. What kind of an example are they presenting to the Cuna? And calling them "savages" was a really weird thing to say about them. Who do they think they are anyway?

<u>*My prejudice and ignorance was showing here. I'm certain these young men were sincere in their efforts of wanting the Cuna to have the kind of faith understood by Christians. The fact of their homosexuality (if in fact they were) had nothing to do with their motive and the work they were doing.*</u>

*   *   *   *   *

With the approaching darkness, the Police granted permission for me to spend the night at the Station. The town of Yaviza did have a single paved sidewalk that became peaceful and quiet after dark. Hardly a human sound was audible above the chatter of the night birds

The night guard at the Police Station was at his desk in the room opposite the entrance, looking bored and probably filling out a meaningless report on something or the other. I asked for, and was granted permission to, sleep at the Station for the night. Pulling two benches together, I made a sleeping space wide and long enough to fit my body and stretch my body full length. The whole place, walls, floor, everything was painted a glaring grey. The whole place smelled of fresh paint, and a bare light bulb hung on a thin wire from the ceiling.

Thoughts of my first love came back to soften my agitated mind; not yet real love, but a true "puppy love"; while at the same time longing for somebody to teach me the Hemmingway things of life. Instead, I had to learn on my own; something that seemed to get harder with each passing year.

The need to learn what I missed from having a fatherless beginning of life helped me to develop a keen sense of observation in order to learn what I could from my environment. It also caused me to want to hide my ignorance. I was ashamed of not knowing even some of the more simple things of life. Strange how the great need to learn from others developed into my biggest blind spot.

For shooting we would borrow a B-B gun and shoot pigeons at night from the back of the Catholic Church steeple; the one at Fourth and Cherry Streets. For fishing we would dive into the muddy waters of the Susquehanna River under the bridge and retrieve lead sinkers, which usually had hooks connected to them. If we were lucky we could sell some of the things to local fishermen, and use the money to buy Hasselback's home-made soft-pretzels (easily the best in the world), or a hot fudge Penn Dairy ice cream sundae with peanuts and whipped cream. Then of course, what summer would be complete without the excitement of stealing cherries

from trees in the backyards of neighbors at six in the morning after sleeping in the city part all night.

We tormented the local winos, threw balloons at passing trucks, and just generally raised hell. But all this ended with the advent of my first love. My puppy love.

I loved Sissy as much as a boy of twelve or thirteen was capable of loving. We would spend much of our classroom time passing notes from classmate to classmate, writing of how much money we might get from our parents for the seven o'clock Friday night movie. It seemed forever for Friday night to come around, but when it did we would buy soft drinks and candy and go to the city park. We always sat on the steps in the darkness, away from the lamp posts, and taught each other how to kiss. In the end, she rejected me for my best friend Ticky Smith. It was an excruciatingly painful time.

The summers that followed that hard-to-forget sadness were spent swimming in the cool waters of the quarry just at the edge of town. The stone quarry filled with fresh water after the owners dug too deep for their stones. It was surrounded with cliffs and ledges from where we would jump, 20, 40, even 100 feet, into the deep water. The best was the "cornfield". The "cornfield" was really a field planted with corn on the top edge of the quarry. The real test of bravery for the "smaller" kids wanting to be a "big" kid was jumping from the cornfield. We would walk back into the cornfield fifteen or twenty yards, run as fast as we could, then jump high over the weeds before seeing the water below. For an instant, it was as if we were suspended in air; neither going up nor going down. Then, like a stone, we would fall the ninety to one hundred feet to the placid water below. What a thrill it was!!!

Those summer days were like paradise on earth. It would be hard to imagine my life without that time. We could walk to the quarry, swim for as long as we wanted, be as courageous as we dared, and return home without adults knowing anything.

Ah, dreamers dream by night in hopes of fulfillment in eternity.

*   *   *   *   *

The hard benches inside the Police Station woke me early in the morning; and I readied myself for the last leg of the gauntlet through the Darien Jungle – to the border at Paya, and into Colombia. The rest, medications, fresh clothing, and hot meals boosted my confidence. I felt strong, and ready to hurdle the remaining seventy-odd miles of the jungle.

It was March ninth. I breathed several deep breaths and readied myself for the rest of the journey with the hope and expectations of a new love.

Chapter 9

Materially, I acquired everything necessary during my stay in Yaviza for the hike up the Tuira River to the border of South America, including cans of sardines and an extra shirt. With several packets of Halezon tablets, antibiotic pills, and even some malaria pills for extra precaution in the saddle bags, I was ready. The equipment was still in fair condition – all considered.

And though I felt confident, another side of me was confused. I had adapted, perhaps my greatest asset, to everything the jungle threw at me. Yet, I continued to feel inadequate around other people, as if they could see some of the things I disliked about myself.

*   *   *   *   *

El Real was five or six miles to the west and south. By going due east from Yaviza after crossing the Chucunaque River, the village of Pinogana could be reached by trekking to the south and east up the Tuira River, bypassing El Real.

Reassured by both the Military Police and Johnny and Alec, an easily accessible road to Pinogana was available once on the opposite bank. I prepared myself to cross the Chucunaque River, which had by now become a familiar landmark, for the last time.

*   *   *   *   *

For the price of two cigarettes I hitched a ride with an old Indian woman across the River and quickly found the much talked about road; it stretched clear and wide in front of me. Enthusiastically, I strutted down the weather-hardened road feeling almost intoxicated as I breathed in deeply with every step. I felt clean and whole again, and happy to be back in the jungle.

Experience taught me this was a typical logger's road; this also made me suspicious. Before realizing it, the jaws of the jungle suddenly closed in on me and I began to feel the familiar terror again. The maze of roads, turned into a maze of trails, and then into barely noticeable paths; trapping me in the near darkness of the green day. Tripping over a near-decayed stump, I fell to the soft jungle floor in a nervous sweat.

Swearing at myself, I could see my dreaded nemesis, the ticks, crawling through the bark, vines, and grass looking for their favorite meal – me. The sweat around my throbbing temples was beginning to dry when I heard the sound of a small, single-engine airplane humming effortlessly overhead. The clear sound of the lightweight craft help me collect my emotionally generated thoughts, as I stretched my neck and lifted my head skyward for a glimpse of the plane. For a second, I caught sight of it before it disappeared, envious of the freedom. I had to get back down to earth and guide myself to somewhere.

Carefully watching each movement of retrieving my body from the jaws of hell, I retraced my steps until finding an open road.

No sooner was the open road reached, when the sound of a rifle shot cracked through the dead silence. This was followed by a quick response of my lungs yelling in a sudden fit of fear, not knowing if I was the intended target. A rustling of the bushes and a few tense seconds later, out popped a laughing frontiersman with a rifle holding a lifeless bird by the claws.

In a not-so-steady voice, but in my most memorized Spanish, I asked him where we were and if he knew of the road to Pinogana. He continued to laugh while giving a "follow me" gesture and started walking in the direction from which I had just come.

Within a mile he stretched his arm and pointed, leading me to a small clear path in a right angle direction. In a minute he was gone, and I was alone again.

Down the trail I passed a patch of old corn and several plots of well-groomed banana trees. Several lumberjacks chopping down cedar trees confirmed that Pinogana was less than an hour away. I encountered four or five hard-looking Panamanians; I sidestepped to allow them to pass. Without exchanging a word, we just stared at each other. They never stopped.

Often I became terrorized by the fear of getting lost, running in all directions to stay on the path. But soon the broad muddy water of the Tuira River was before me, blindly reflecting the sunlight and warming my face. There was no sign of people.

Before the sweat on my brow had dried, a tiny piraqua was heading toward me. In it were a slight Panamanian mother and her small daughter. Seeing me, they stopped. Repeating "Pinogana" several times, the mother nodded and agreed to take me there. It was probably the world's smallest piraqua. It was only ten feet long and barely wide enough to fit my narrow buttocks and my equipment. Though small in stature and body frame, the Negro woman paddled with skill and determination against the Tuira current toward Pinogana.

The scene was one of quiet serenity that could have been duplicated in most parts of the world and at any time in history. The banks of the river could offer no clues of a where or when. The mother wore very simple cotton clothes; the daughter nothing except a beaded necklace. The dug-out canoe could have come from a tree near the Nile, the Amazon, even the Mississippi a hundred or a thousand years ago; except, that is, for the sight of one time-space traveler.

Thirty minutes of daydreaming came to a sudden end when Pinogana was sighted a few hundred yards up the river to the right.

On arrival, a small band of energetic children swarmed around the canoe laughing and pointing as I unloaded my equipment. The mother refused payment for transporting me, but did permit me to give the child a few coins (less than fifty cents) stashed in my saddle bags. Spirit-like, she pointed the canoe away from Pinogana and paddled downstream, her daughter smiling with a handful of American coins.

The children of Pinogana nearly dragged me to the only public store in town, and introduced me to Elcier; the leading citizen of the village's fifty or sixty inhabitants. He was a tall, broad-shouldered and intelligent man who spoke very good English; he had also worked in the Canal Zone.

Elcier bluntly stated few canoes passed Pinogana heading east, and knew of no passable trails going to Paya. I could stay with him until catching a canoe to Boca de Cupe – about twenty-five miles upstream. After that, I may be able to walk from village to village to reach the border village of Paya; and from there into Colombia.

*   *   *   *   *

For two days and nights, Elcier unselfishly provided me with two hot meals a day and a dry place to sleep. But it was the sleeping, or attempt to sleep, that became the hair-raising experience.

Elcier said I was to sleep in his generator shack located a few hundred feet from his house at the edge of town and on the fringe of the jungle. The generator produced enough electricity for one building – Elciers' home – and was promptly switched off at nine o'clock each night.

He led the way, and I, with my equipment and machete, was happy knowing my sleep would be in the prone position, inside a dry building, and alone. Little did I know the shack was host to other, foreboding creatures?

Unlocking and pushing open the warped door; we each struck a match and found the stub of a candle amid a lump of uneven wax stuck to the floor a few feet from the door. Elcier excused the poor conditions, bid me good evening, closed the door and left. I was alone in the room, left with only the silence and flickering candlelight. It was just me and my shadow. As if someone were listening, I quietly unrolled the sleeping gear on the dry wooden floor, littered with dust, tiny feathers, and dung droplets. Thinking I had slept in a lot worse conditions, I sat down, leaning near the candle, and began writing a recap of the day's events in my cherished notebook by the dim light.

Just as the writing was about finished, a corpulent animal scurried between my hand and the candle just inches from my lowered face. It was a RAT, a huge brown RAT so large its thick whiskers showed clearly sprouting from its nose! It was as large as a house cat, and could probably devour one in minutes.

I bolted upright in a battle-ready position with the machete held high in combat readiness.

But nothing happened! The rat scampered through a hole in the wood wall; silence returned, save for the distant crickets and bullfrogs. The light from the swaying candle wick showed my bloated silhouette on the uneven wall to my right like an oversized Hunchback of Notre Dame. Looking silly but feeling uneasy, I knew I had to sleep as close as possible to the candle in hopes that the heat and light would fend off the rodents.

Lying on the right side, my ear was near the floor and began to hear the occasional sounds of the long-clawed rats slipping across the hard floor. The thought of a diseased rat's teeth eating at my flesh caused my eyelids to remain locked open as my eyes darted about chasing each sound, real or imagined. With extremely discomforting thoughts, I began a board by board inspection of the entire room. I covered, clogged and jammed the holes with anything available, hoping to seal off any rat entrance or exit; I returned to my blanket hoping for some sleep.

The sound of simmering candle wax brought my consciousness to a higher level a short while later. The wick, lying in a pool of melted wax, crackled for oxygen, trying to sustain light. Its spark repeatedly went from very bright to near darkness.

Just then I heard another rat running from behind to the front of me. He tried to get through a hole clogged with an oily rag but couldn't. Stopping, the animal jumped back and over my hands. Instinctively I sprang up and chased it with the machete to the opposite corner.

The grotesque-looking rodent, nearly as large as a garbage dump tom-cat, displayed large dust balls stuck on one whisker; probably speared as a result of having to alter its travel pattern. Smoothly it dashed to the next corner and raised its back in a high curve. The predator bared its teeth and emitted a sharp hissing sound, momentarily stopping me and starting a nervous jitter.

In that moment of hesitation, the rat sprinted between my spread legs, spinning me around. Turning, I instinctively slammed the machete in the rat's anticipated path.

Success!

The machete struck diagonally across the animal's hind end breaking its back. It squealed and contorted its upper body in a vain attempt to elude the inevitable. I struck it a second time. Then, with all my weight pushing down on the handle of the machete, the dull tip of the metallic blade pierced the skin until I felt the bones break in its neck. A small pool of dark blood gathered near the head gash.

Dead!

Stepping back, my feelings of victory soon changed to perplexity. Why did I have to kill the rat? Why be the taker of life? One rat wouldn't make a difference in that rodent-infested building, in the rodent-infested jungle, or in the rodent-infested world.

And, now that it was dead, what was I to do with the corpse?

Dragging the bleeding and lifeless body out of the shack and to the nearby jungle, I slung the animal, easily fourteen to sixteen inches long, as hard and far as I could into the darkened jungle fortress. From the light of the half-moon I saw the blood dripping from its mouth; I saw a hanging tongue too, still in defiance. Reluctantly I returned to the shack, wiped up the blood, and wrapped myself in the sleeping gear in a corner, praying only for survival.

The activity of the rats didn't stop because one of their own had been killed. Throughout the night, more rats sneaked around the inside of the shack nipping at my sleeping gear and boots; they dispersed after I slammed the machete aimlessly onto the wooden floor with a very loud bang. This behavior continued until the first hint of dawn. I got maybe an hour of sleep.

*   *   *   *   *

After the surroundings became more visible, I rolled up the sleeping gear and walked to Elcier's makeshift wharf to watch the sun come up, and looked for a passing piraqua heading up the Tuira River.

I sat on the rickety wharf, legs hanging over the end; boots barely skimming the surface of the seemingly motionless water. Passing birds flapped their wings in complacent harmony only a few feet above the water's surface. Occasionally a small fish would break the glassy water, sending rippling waves into the universe. Sphinx-like I remained stationary on the timeworn wharf, eyes fixed on the river with a mind galloping over the sand-dunes of time, concentrating on that one canoe that would carry me upriver to the Promised Land.

*   *   *   *   *

The air along the Tuira River became uncomfortably heavy. I was sweating without moving a muscle, and it was still the early part of the day. But the need to be moving – going somehow – toward Boca de Cupe or Paya was tempered by the remembrance of horrors past.

Elcier reminded me that Boca de Cupe was six hours upriver by a motor powered boat and anyone hoping to get there by sunset would need to pass his wharf here in Pinogana by midday.

Feeling dejected and with stiff and cramped muscles, I slowly raised my body from the time-worn wharf and carried the equipment back to the generator shack.

With a half of day and nothing to do, no books to read, nothing to write in the notebook, and nowhere to go, and like a moth drawn to heat, I ambled down a well-cultivated path at the south end of the village.

I thought how wonderful it would be to live in the succulent jungle as a "natural man", to roam freely seeking only food, shelter, and the few necessities of life, like our ancestors of thousands of years. I wanted to leave everything behind and go "back to nature". Weird thoughts crept into my brain, like to just continue walking down the trail without care of where it was going or how to survive. I was literally running down a nearly unused trail of the main path going in the opposite direction from the sanctuary and security of Pinogana - and had no idea why. Chopping wildly at pressing foliage, my heart pulsated from the runaway emotions of an excited mind.

Just as impulsive, I screeched to a sudden stop. Was I going mad?

For an interim I just stood there, arms akimbo, shaking my head in disbelief. In a moment of self-realization, I made a conscious commitment to more and more self-mastery.

I twisted my neck and looked in the direction of the village, then turned and looked at the maze of green emptiness. Then with one powerful aggressive swipe of the machete, I neatly severed a restraining vine and strode back to the village.

*   *   *   *   *

After another nearly sleepless night and doing battle with the rats in the infested generator shack, I posted myself once again at daybreak by the lonely pier hoping for a ride. The Rio Tuira was well-traveled that day, but alas; no boats were going as far upriver as Paya, or even Boca de Cupe.

And again I returned my equipment to the generator shack after mid-day.

I was in the store talking with Elcier when his teenage son came running in with the news that a late-in-the-day piraqua was motoring for Boca de Cupe and could spare the space for an additional passenger.

Leaping from the seat, I dashed to the shack for my gear and hurried to the wharf.

After a short but fierce bargain, the owner of the boat agreed to take me along for the price of three American dollars, with the provision that I assist in pushing the canoe or otherwise help with the chores.

Promising to send a postcard from South America, I said goodbye to Elcier, his family, and everyone who came to the riverbank; at last I was on my way to Boca de Cupe.

It was a long, deep piraqua with six Panamanians and piles of household items and equipment loaded near the middle. Strapped to the back was an old Mercury outboard; probably in the range of 25 horsepower. A prematurely aging fair-skinned man sitting in front of me complained hourly of my leaning on his burlap bag squashing his oranges. But it was a six hour trip so I paid little attention to him and dozed often.

After several hours of steady upstream driving, the owner steered the canoe to a large, brown, sandy bank and stopped the engine. Accompanied by three fellow travelers, he ran into the trees and returned after only a few minutes. Each man carried a large watermelon. Soon slices of delicious tasting, thirst quenching, red watermelon were passed around to all.

This was the only excitement of the whole trip to Boca de Cupe. Not once was it necessary for any of us to get out and push the canoe.

As expected, the canoe didn't arrive until well after the sunset. By the dimming light, I could see Boca de Cupe consisted of merely fourteen or fifteen poorly thrown together houses on stilts in a row near the river. The bare clay ground connecting them formed a semblance of a street.

Near the center of the "town" was what appeared to be a dance floor; it was protected from the weather by a make-shift roof of bamboo and palm leaves. It seemed to be public property, so I strung my hammock between the two pillars supporting the roof and prepared for, and hoped for, sleep. Still, my metabolism raced with the excitement of having reached the next village; I was one step closer to Colombia.

Before retiring, I noticed with humor a donkey tied to a post near the shack where I was about to sleep. The smile soon turned to anguish after the few oil lanterns in the village were blown out and the black night surrounded the tiny village.

I snugly rolled on my right side in the hammock and prepared for a long night of uninterrupted rest, free of rats. Suddenly out of the darkness of the night came the shrieking cry of the donkey: HEE-HAW, HEE-HAW, HEE-HAW, HEE-HAW! He would *hee* with each inhale, and *haw* with each exhale. I jerked upright with what sounded like the wailing of some unknown being from outer space. The hee-hawing soon tapered off and lost its piercing quality ending with a very definite puff, until only the sound of the croaking frogs and the crickets could be heard in the thick silence of the humid night.

After sleeping for less than an hour, the donkey repeated the nerve-wracking braying with the same strength and duration. I was jolted out of a dreamy sleep and shocked into a twisted sense of reality. His cries seemed as if in despair, as if looking for or searching for freedom from the retaining rope holding him to the wooden post.

But his problems were not my problems. I cursed at the donkey, ass, mule, demon or whatever kind of animal he was; I wished a million maggots would feast upon his dead and cold body. What the hell was a donkey doing in the middle of the jungle anyway? What prompted him was a mystery, and the long-eared animal would send shrilling vocal sounds cascading through the night once or sometimes twice an hour.

By morning my nerves were like a mish-mash of electric wires shocking me with each irregular sound touching my naked ear drums.

It was another night of disturbed sleep.

*   *   *   *   *

The hazy morning sunlight saw me rummaging through the village of Boca de Cupe looking for information to feed the hunger of getting to Paya and a run to the border.

The name of Paya had been branded in my mind from the very beginning. I could skillfully pronounce and spell it backward, locate its position on the map without hesitation, and continue many fantasies of what it possibly looked like. It seemed so close. The vision was clearer.

Several villagers told me there was no jungle trail leading there, and the only way to Paya was up the Tuira. One elder said the best possibility would be to go upriver to Púcuro – an Indian village eight or ten miles upriver – and from there a trail to Paya was possible. Boca de Cupe, he said, was the last Panamanian outpost before the border. Both Púcuro and Paya were Cuna villages, although there was a military office in Paya for checking credentials of anyone crossing the border in either direction.

So I again sat by the riverbank hoping for a canoe, and fighting the need for sleep.

Since being in the jungle, I'd learned to not trust the directional information given by anyone farther than the line-of-sight. Everyone wanted to be helpful, but usually gave misinformation about how to get from place to place.

When the citizens of Boca de Cupe realized my condition – especially poor financial situation – most offered food, clothes, and a place to sleep, despite their own poverty-stricken life. They were obviously poor, living off the land, and had little cash money and few commodities.

Their kindness reopened an old wound experienced since leaving California. It was a sore on a level of awareness just below the conscious, a dilemma actually. Was I to take care of myself, or help others? Tons of people had helped me along the way and I couldn't pay – or repay - them for their offerings. I had the money, but needed to keep much for the South American destination; and to be able to return stateside. What to do? Every time and nearly every person encountered, I was forced to make a decision; decisions, decisions, and more decisions.

In essence, I felt as if I were becoming parasitic. I didn't even know the Spanish or Cuna languages well enough to express and explain my feelings toward them. To what degree of a parasite had I become? True, most of the people of the Darien didn't expect any payment or anything in return; perhaps they were even insulted by the offer. But the recent experiences of travel from village to village caused me to expect food, shelter, and information from whomever was in the village.

I knew then I didn't want to go through the rest of my life feeling this way. There was a new sense arising, of the need for receiving *and* giving back; with an ultimate balance between a healthy self-care and a sincere unselfishness to help others.

My tormented mind had quieted with a light sleep as I rested against a large banyan tree, but was suddenly shaken from the slumber by a huge black hand touching my right shoulder. Befuddled, I stared blankly into the man's eyes, eyes surrounded by majestic skin so black there seemed to be shades of purple reflected in the afternoon sun.

Showing a perfect set of small white teeth (a rarity where sugar cane is in abundance), the man smiled and quietly stated he was Alexander Edwards and would pole me in his canoe to Púcuro in the morning – if I so desired. From there, he said, he knew of a trail leading to Paya. Shyly, he requested cash for his services while at the same time placing a bunch of ripe bananas on my lap.

He had fathered seven children and said two American dollars would mean a lot to him. He and his family lived on a small banana plantation next to Boca de Cupe and were obviously in desperate need of money. Wanting to hug him, I jumped to my feet and shook hands to confirm the deal. We would get under way at the first trace of daylight.

The maddening mule made certain I was ready to travel the next morning. A surprised Mr. Edwards saw me packed and ready to leave when he arrived with one of his younger sons. Together they would pole their canoe to Púcuro, some fifteen miles upstream on a tributary of the Tuira named Rio Tapalisa. We positioned ourselves in the narrow canoe and pushed into the dense fog enveloping the quiet river, leaving the donkey and Boca de Cupe in our rear-view mirror.

Mr. Edwards, a lanky six-foot man, pulled most of the weight from the forward peak of the piraqua with a costumed-carved pole. His son, named Jesus and exactly half his father's size, eagerly assisted from the stern using a much smaller pole. The going was slow but steady, highlighted only by an embarrassed Jesus who, after changing positions with his father, slipped off the peak of the piraqua into the Tuira. After the third fall, the young man resigned himself to the role of helper. But, they were a good father-son team and kept the canoe moving upriver even against the most choppy rapids. I greatly admired them.

We finally arrived in Púcuro in the early hours of the afternoon. I was surprised to see it only consisted of three or four Cuna families in huts scattered about in the neatly kept village.

Mr. Edwards ducked into one of the huts and quickly returned with their chief, a short stocky man with a gold nose ring. The two led me to the river's edge and pointed to an opening in the trees on the opposite bank and repeated the word "Paya" "Paya" "Paya" over and over again.

My map shows Púcuro on the right bank of the Tapalisa River. And Paya was also shown to be on the right bank of the Paya River, which was part of the Tuira River – at least according to this map. If I crossed the river I could be walking in the wrong direction. Somewhat mystified and doubtful, I decided to take the chief's advice.

The chief returned to the village and the Edwards poled me across to the opposite side of the river. I gave him the two dollars, we all shook hands, and they were soon on their way home, leaving me with the thought Mr. Edwards was still the darkest skinned man I'd ever seen.

Perhaps the trail would dissect with the river after a few miles and reveal a clear trail to Paya, I hoped. But I really didn't care as I walked, almost ran, down the trail into the thicket with my mixed feelings of secure aloneness and the need to share.

I was at least heading in the right direction and getting closer and closer to the coveted South America. Everything seemed to be going my way – finally. The lithe branches and succulent plant stems fell obediently after each single swipe of the machete, honed into razor sharpness during the idle days along the river. My health was improving and my mind was fanciful, allowing me to laugh, scream, and skip along – anything.

In my childish display of folly and merriment, I decided to indulge in food after walking less than a mile. In Yaviza, I learned how to make a sardines sandwich; a most delicious "Sardine Submarine". By first delicately slicing open one of the rolls of narrow bread carried in the saddle bags, neatly opening the oval shaped can of sardines with a P-38, and gently placing each juicy, moist sardine inside, I would finish it off by pouring the extra tomato sauce and oil onto the absorbing bread. In monotonous mouth-grinding motion, the slow eating allowed my sensitive taste buds to enjoy the sweetness to the fullest. Squeezing the rounded ends of the bread rolls I'd neatly wipe the elongated can of the remaining oil and red sauce. The tin can would be filled with water and the contents drained into my mouth in an effort to get every possible nutritional richness and joy out of the experience.

The eating orgy climaxed with a thorough finger licking.

My lust fulfilled, I jaunted happily down the jungle trail, confident in my ability to walk the remaining distance into Colombia without difficulty or delay. The experience gained after nearly a month in the Darien and the knowledge that the goal was within reach raised my spirits and boosted my morale.

What I'd seen, what I'd done… I felt something new; an unbelievable emotion. It felt an uplifting sensation. But in the end, it was ineffable. Everything seemed so uncomplicated.

Hey, maybe Kerouac had it right after all!

*   *   *   *   *

I don't remember hearing the thunder or seeing the lightening as a large bank of rolling black clouds darkened the usually bright sky. Just as suddenly, heavy drops of rain began falling, pelting me and the jungle foliage. At first only a few drops ricocheted off the nearby broad brittle leaves. Then, as if an explosion had opened the thick clouds, falling water came rushing down from the sky in a steady pour. I tried hugging a tree, but it proved useless. So I just continued walking down the misty, soggy trail.

Then as quickly as it began, the cloudburst ended, and a few minutes later the sun was again shining brightly overhead. In the distance the dark billowing clouds remained for several hours, an ominous reminder the rainy season was approaching. It would be a vast understatement to say I didn't want to be caught in the Darien Jungle during the monsoons.

*   *   *   *   *

A few miles past Púcuro, I noticed the sound of gushing water rapids, and it drew my eyes to the right bank of the water.

There I saw a few small Indian huts with a few Cuna mingling about, and guessed it to be only the temporary home of some wandering Indians. I avoided them and continued marching down the path, still wanting to do everything on my own.

The trail followed the river past the Indians' huts for a short while before departing on its own course, leaving me alone in the jungle.

Nothing escaped the thorough rainy downpour. Removing all the dust and dirt from the luscious plant life, it created a sparkling green spectacle unparalleled by any manmade greenhouse I'd ever seen. It lit up my imagination to a kaleidoscope of changing patterns with each and every step.

But the rainy season was coming.

The aesthetic excitement began to subside with the realization that the trail was gradually veering westward. It was growing late in the afternoon and the sun would be soon setting. But I was walking directly toward the sun, in the *opposite* direction for Colombia.

Goosebumps of fear rippled up my back and neck at the thought of again being lost in the jungle. I pulled out the compass from the saddle-bags hoping for an accurate account of my direction. But the glass top of the compass showed nothing but moisture because it was full of water, rendering it a better leveling tool than a directional finder. Violently shaking the compass several times, the validating sounds of the sloshing water caused me to throw the worthless piece of junk into the air off to the left of me as hard and far as my arm allowed. An immediate shock ran down my arm from the excessive sling, as the compass was heard hitting the different types of foliage and fell to the jungle floor a hundred feet away.

I didn't know where I was or what to do. I *did* know that under no circumstances would I return to Púcuro, or any other of the villages already visited. On the other hand, I didn't want to head off in an easterly course through pathless jungle; the obstacles, as I well knew, were torturous. Yet the stagnating thoughts of inertia made me nervous.

So, head leaning forward and jaw set tight, I charged forward on the same trail cursing under my breath for putting myself in such a ridiculous predicament. I walked and walked, vainly searching for signs of a path heading easterly; even southward. But the longer I walked, the more westerly was the trail.

As I walked, several small streams flowed downward to my left, confirming the fact of my being without direction. Occasionally, a stream would be on the right. But if this were the good trail, all rivers or creeks should be flowing to my right. It was as if I were going around in circles, not knowing any of the names of the creeks or rivers.

The sky was beginning to show sure signs of lateness as I came upon a large creek, whose name I couldn't possibly know. Near the water's edge was a bunch of banana trees. I decided this was the end of the trail for today; no more traveling in the wrong direction. A feeling of defeat enshrouded me. Physical exhaustion and low morale put me in a sour mood, not caring if I progressed another yard. With the bananas for food and the river for water, I made camp, vowing to not budge another inch until I knew exactly where I was going and how to get there.

Chapter 10

I awoke the next morning in a state of deep dilemma, compounded by a thumping headache.

Where was my campsite located on the map, and in which direction would I have to travel to arrive at the Panamanian-Colombia border town of Paya? It was March 14th, 1965, and I was again hopelessly lost after twenty-eight days in the Darien Jungle. I wanted to keep moving in order to shrink the distance between my present location and the elusive South American border. The only means of direction I had was watching the sun rise in the east – a fact which really didn't help much.

After walking nearly eight hours the day before, following the departure of Mr. Edwards at Púcuro, I could easily have traveled the eight or ten miles distance to Paya. But Paya was nowhere in sight, and I had no clue of how to get there. My mind was a mess. The map was of little help because it displayed none of the detailed tributaries, and I had crossed so many creeks and/or rivers…

Of only one thing was I certain: all creeks and rivers flowed in a southerly direction, back to Púcuro. But I still had no clue as to where I was – on the map *or* on the ground.

But where <u>are</u> we in the universe?

*   *   *   *   *

After the thin foggy mist cleared from the running water, the day brightened up and raised my temperament. The sun quickly burst through the early morning clouds drying my damp clothes and equipment. The only decision I could make was to prepare a breakfast using the acquired skills learned over the past weeks. My hope, also, was for the food to thwart the headache pain and put an end to procrastination; one of my long-held, hard-headed, character flaws.

As it turned out, the breakfast was my most elaborate meal prepared during the entire jaunt through the Darien. It consisted of roasted *plantano* bananas, baked potato roots, and a couple of small fried fish. The bananas required a very long time to cook due to their greenness, the potatoes were from a special plant but tasted like Idaho spuds to me, (a young Pinogana boy showed me this secret, and I discovered that nearly the entire jungle floor in most areas was filled with them), and the tiny fish were easily trapped in my mosquito net. The fish were tasty, but with hundreds of sharp bones. Overall, it was a fantastic and satisfying meal.

Afterward, I built a simple lean-to hut from some nearby bamboo poles and palm leaves and neatly laid my gear inside. Needing a bath, I undressed and waded into the cool shallow stream. Placing the thin bar of soap inside one of the new stockings I scrubbed my body all over. It felt good, and helped the blood in my body return to normal circulation, as I sat naked by the still burning fire softly rubbing the soothing salve into the infected bug-bites.

By now, I was beginning to not care whether or not I left the campsite. I was beginning to feel comfortably at home.

After dressing and stringing up the hammock, I dozed into a sweet sleep even though it was not yet noontime. I didn't know how long I slept. When I was finally awakened, I woke to what became my best stroke of luck since being in the Darien Jungle. My period of indecision was over.

*   *   *   *   *

*Here I am on this luck thing again. Luck may infer some reference to being "chosen". But I find it difficult to accept some sort of **favoritism** by the rulers of the universe. There surely must be accidents of time and space – a misstep here, and auto accident there. But can it be an accident when it comes to the meeting and interactions of people? And what about predestination or foreordination?*

Was it luck that placed me on the edge of the Bayano River twenty-five days before to be picked up by a passing canoe after only fifteen minutes of waiting? Was it luck that helped me find the roads of the logging camps on the Rio Canazas, and then again on the Chucunaque? Was it luck that caused a canoe to come down the Chucunaque at the exact moment when I was completely exhausted and near death after losing the balsa raft just nine days before? And again, was it luck that a hunter happened to find me wandering around the jungle trying to find the real road to Pinogana? And now, was it luck that placed me next to the rippling creek?

I think not!

In a state of semi-sleep, I thought I was imagining two voices close by speaking to each other in an inquisitive manner. I sat up and actually saw two Latin men walking through the shallow water at the creek's edge. They were definitely walking straight toward me. They looked Panamanian and were carrying light back-packs and a machete in hand, and had obviously been in motion for a long time; as sweat showed on their foreheads and on their clothing.

My surprise was clearly displayed. I just stood there waiting for them to approach me, not knowing whether to laugh or cry, be friendly or suspicious.

We greeted each other in Spanish, and after using the few words I had come to memorize, we were able to piece together a conversation. They first asked the questions, also in a surprised manner, and wanted to know which country I was from, how I got this far into the jungle, and exactly where was I going. I told them, or tried to tell them, everything, including my hopes of finding the village of Paya in order to get into Colombia.

Then I asked the questions. They answered they had walked from El Real and Yaviza and were also heading to Paya, causing my heart to leap with excitement. They admitted to being native Colombians, not Panamanians, who were attempting to get back to their homes in Turbo.

Still I couldn't believe my luck!

Turbo was exactly where the Pan-American Highway resumed, and was the best case scenario as the first arrival city. I literally jumped several inches off the sand when they said I could follow them to their homes in Turbo. Before another word was spoken, I haphazardly ran about the small campsite throwing my equipment together for the march to Paya and on to Turbo, Colombia, afraid the men would leave me behind.

As I packed the gear, the fragmented conversation continued. Via broken English and Spanish, sign language, and body gestures I gathered they were trappers coming to the Darien Jungle for animal skins and returning to Colombia to sell them for big profit. (I never actually saw any of the skins.) The men were hesitant and didn't want to accept my story of walking all the way from Panama City, which was of course, not true. But an explanation of the motorcycle journey into the jungle, leaving it, getting to where I was, became too cumbersome and difficult to communicate and translate.

They insisted upon seeing my passport, I believe, to be certain I was American. Without ever opening the blue/green colored cover, the sight of the American passport impressed them. In fact, they seemed overly impressed. The two became very emphatic in their desire to have me as a traveling companion. All the while, the men perpetrated an air of secretiveness with a touch of intrigue.

We would be in Paya within eight hours, they assured me, before dark. And, to top that, we would be in Turbo, Colombia within two and a half days. It was hard to believe! It seemed like a dream! Two and a half days – only two and a half more days – of perseverance and my troubles would be over. What a deal!

All I had to do was to forget the pain, forget my bone-thin body, forget the agonizing thoughts and feelings for just this last short period of time. Self-doubt weaseled its way inside, but having someone to follow bolstered my confidence. If only I could close my eyes and be in Turbo. I could image what it looked like. But I knew I had to slug it out for two or three more days in the belly – no, the lower bowels - of this jungle. I prayed for a quick passage of time; I also readied my gear for the big push.

* * * * *

One of the men wore a thin mustache and had very light colored skin. I never did learn either of their names, so I call the mustachioed one Pablo. The other man was shorter and darker of skin color and without facial hair, and I called him Tomo. Pablo was clearly the leader and seemed to laugh at nearly everything anyone said, including his own statements, a characteristic that became annoying over time. In contrast, the young Tomo spoke only when spoken to, smiled little and laughed even less, but had a look of endearment in his eyes. After a few hundred yards on the trail, the chatter came to a sudden stop.

It quickly became obvious that these men were serious hikers. They set a pace of long fast strides down the trail; they never stopped and they never looked back. We walked in single file, with Tomo leading, Pablo in the middle, and me bringing up the rear. And, ironically, we started walking down the trail in the same direction I had walked the day before, along the same path I swore never to return. After about two hours of walking without let-up we came to the same river – the Tapalisa River – and the same spot I had passed before.

Then to my stunned disbelief, the men led me through the water and to the small group of Cuna huts. Unburdening myself of the heavy gear, I admitted to a gross error of judgment: the small settlement I saw from across the river shortly after leaving Mr. Edwards, and where I now stood, was the *real* Púcuro. The settlement Mr. Edwards had led me to previously was only that of a small group of wandering Indians, without a name, or even the title "village". If I had just initially crossed the river to investigate, two days of torture and dilly-dallying around could possibly have been saved; and, I may have already arrived in Paya. In spite of myself, I realized the need for assistance from these Indians I so smugly rejected before.

We stayed in Púcuro for half an hour eating lunch. I made another one of the delicious "submarine sandwiches", and ate a few overly ripe bananas offered by the leader of the Cuna. Knowing I was an American, this Cuna was constantly engaging me in conversation. My two companions managed to talk their way into a bowl of rice and deer meat, but they did pay a small fee in Panamanian money for it.

From the outside of one of the huts, I saw an Indian woman sitting on the dirt floor weaving a mat; a child of two or three years old explored nearby. Suddenly, the child stopped playing and began to cry. Just as quickly, the mother placed her hand behind the child's black-haired head, pulled the little-one to her bare breast. The baby stopped crying and began suckling. I'm not certain why I remembered this incident. It wasn't unusual. The sight of a Cuna mother with thin legs, a fat belly, and low-hanging breasts thrusting the child's mouth to her nipple somehow remained a long retained memory.

Interesting, isn't it, what we remember or don't remember as we go through life?

The sun was high, and the jungle air was baking-hot when we left Púcuro. Shortly after the village disappeared from sight, I came to realize that without the guidance of Pablo and Tomo it would have been impossible for me to have found the trail to Paya.

They led me under fallen trees, over rotted logs, through shallow creeks and into jungle brush as thick as any I'd seen. The trail was so distorted and thick with foliage in most areas that only a very experienced traveler could "see" the path. As the sun crossed from the top of the speckled sky toward the horizon, we never stopped our rapid pace, never stopped for water, never slowed for a rest. Silently we progressed toward the end of Panamanian territory, our soaked and salted clothing clinging to our skins.

As the sky began to gray, I sensed the nearness of Paya and knew the distance between our location and South America was rapidly shrinking. My goal was within reach; only a little while longer; I would be in Paya before nightfall.

*   *   *   *   *

The desperately sinking sun was trying to cling to the horizon when our three steaming bodies stopped beside a few Indian huts to the left of the gushing Paya River.

Across the river stood a small wood building, representing the last outpost of civilization in Panama. It was Paya. After all the pain and suffering, joy and exhilaration, I didn't know what to expect, but seeing Paya from across the river was the biggest anticlimax of the journey. Paya consisted of one poorly constructed building with an aluminum sheeted roof and half a dozen thatched-roof huts nearby. I couldn't believe this was the Paya I had heard about, the Paya I'd dreamed about, the citadel burning in my mind since entering the Darien. The aluminum panels glimmered in the setting sun, the only sign of any civilization.

Visually following the river upstream, and adding insult to injury, nothing but rising mountainous jungle could be seen, thickened by masses of dense trees and plant life, worse than anything I'd seen thus far. So, not only was Paya just an outpost, but the jungle beyond looked impenetrable. And I had been foolish enough to believe Paya was the end of my hardships, the end of the jungle, and the end of my worries.

I couldn't have been more wrong! The mountainous jungle just continued on and on without heeding man-made lines on a map.

Meanwhile, the two Colombians ducked into one of the Cuna huts for what looked like intense bargaining before forging our way across the choppy Paya River to the aluminum building.

Once there, we were promptly met by two members of *La Guradia*, the right arm of the Panamanian Military Police. Pablo did some very fast talking, most of which I was unable to understand. He consistently pointed toward me and laughed. Somehow, I had the distinct feeling I was being *used*, for what I didn't know; perhaps as their easy passage into Colombia. Tomo didn't say a word, and neither showed a passport.

The two *La Guardians* and Colombians disappeared for a few minutes, and when they returned all were smiling. The guards led me through the near darkness into the lamp-lit building where they thoroughly and meticulously inspected every article and stitch of material I carried, probably looking for contraband. Satisfying themselves that all was in order, they released me to the company of the Colombians in the thatched hut next door. Before leaving the guardhouse, I ask the population of Paya – six *La Guardians* and three Cuna families.

Pablo, Tomo, and I prepared our hammocks for sleep. Tired from the day's long walk, I was feeling irritated and confused, but not really knowing what I had expected. Sleep, however, would not have come too easily had I known the morning would bring more confusion and mystery.

* * * * *

Under the cloak of the cool misty dawn, and at least an hour before sunrise, the Colombians woke me to the movement of my swinging hammock. Shaking my bed with one hand, Tomo held a straightened finger to his lips in a sign of silence and motioned to ready myself for traveling. Unsure of what was going on, I obeyed his orders.

They too rolled their sleeping gear smoothly and collected their belongings. Both men turned their heads quickly toward me with each sound accidentally made in the semi-darkness, emitting a shushing sound in my direction. They waited impatiently until I was ready, and then led me away from our hut and past the wood guard house and into the shadowy forest.

Nobody knew we were leaving Paya, and we told nobody we were leaving. We just left *en silencio*.

Once a comfortable distance from the outpost, Pablo let out a long, loud laugh that echoed through the silent trees and rolling hills in concert with a few chirping birds. This explosion of laughter lasted only a short while, however, as the sounds rolled down the hills in the direction of Paya causing the men to turn and dash – almost run – up the trail and into the wooded mountains, me trailing close behind. My passport was never stamped.

* * * * *

Like two well lubricated and synchronized machines, the men before me walked and walked with me in tow. Never had I sweated so much. The salty fluid seemed to spurt out of my pores in a continuous stream as though my blood had turned to water. Up one hill and down another, we went higher into the mountains. The water of every stream gushed down the mountainside as if it were shot from a gun. With gallons of cool available water, I drank freely in an effort to maintain a high fluid level, easily consuming a half quart of water each time Pablo and Tomo stopped, which wasn't often. I drank at least a canteen of water per hour, and the Halazone tablets were getting in short supply. Just about every inch of clothing was completely soaked from sweat, and even my boots showed the dark stains of sweat through the heavy leather and canvas.

Each time the two men slowed their pace or hesitated for a moment, I hoped for a rest to unburden myself from the heavy gear, if only for a few minutes.

This reminded me of the "forced marches" we had in the military. We'd walk 15, sometimes 20 miles a day with full gear, just to get us "in shape".

But they continued on and on, pumping their legs up and down as if their lives depended on it; and maybe they did. I followed behind, determined to keep pace just as I did in the U.S. military.

They were my escape ticket. I refused to let them out of my sight, even for a minute.

*   *   *   *   *

About midday, I was surprised to see two Cuna Indians standing at a junction in the trail, not more than a few yards in front of us. The Indians were carrying large woven baskets on their backs held in place by wide straps across their foreheads. They were typical Cuna, with only a small cloth around their waist, and looked to be straining under the weight of their baskets. Upon a closer look, the baskets were nearly empty.

My initial reaction turned to suspicion as the Colombians and the Indians greeted each other as if friends, and sat on the ground for a whispered conversation apart from me. After a short discussion, the Indians joined us; all following the trail upward and eastward.

We five presented a motley picture. And though I felt a little uneasy in the presence of these strange and whispering men, I could not help but chuckle at the variety of cultures: Darien

Cuna, Colombians, and an American. Naturally, I was the only one suffering from the jungle's harshness.

After several hours of silent walking, our group separated. The Indians departed on another trail, but not before another secretive meeting in the bushes a few yards in front of me. They tried to conceal the exchange of a small package wrapped in dark brown paper from one of the Indians to Pablo, but I saw it. The Cuna then headed on a more easterly path and were soon out of sight. The word "Playita" was spoken, but I assumed it was a variation on Paya. I never saw them again and never saw another Darien Jungle Cuna.

After that, Pablo's attitude changed and became less cocky and more solemn.

* * * * *

The hours of meditative walking continued, but the pace slowed slightly as we neared the top of the mountain range. The thigh muscles in my legs were feeling the burning effect of the strenuous uphill walking, even after all the walking already under my belt.

I tried diverting my thoughts to the rolling hills. The ever-changing face of the jungle had changed again. Now it was a soft, fresh look, dotted with taller and more scattered trees, a real wooded forest. The dense, dark shrubbery was conspicuously absent. Only small spots of tall grass and a few budding trees marred the view of the surrounding tall trees standing like pillars holding up the sky.

The air was cool and the sunlight showed through large cracks in the low-hanging branches like transparent beams of yellow steel. An occasional animal was heard scurrying away. Birds were all around, flitting about from tree to tree, as if they were following us. A soft breeze blew in light persistence, buffeting my face and I felt in tune with nature; mother nature's son.

To add to the fantasy rapture, Pablo and Tomo stopped by the trail on top of a high mountain to look back at the sweeping view of the valley below. They knew of fresh water a few hundred feet below, off to the left side of the trail, and beckoned me to follow. Always ready to indulge in water, I eagerly followed the men down the clay path until it ended at a small stream and moss covered rocks.

Following the stream downward, we soon came upon a beautiful series of musical waterfalls pouring out of the mountain rocks. Enchanted, I stood there transfixed by the total beauty. A ray of sunlight pierced the spray of one of the smaller falls creating a rainbow, nature's rebuttal to the artist.

Mimicking the others, I quickly undressed and showered under one of the several high waterfalls; sharing my thin slice of soap with them. I wished to tell them of my adventures, my hopes and my desires, not caring if they were thieves or smugglers. But I was unable to do so, and returned my attention to the surrounding beauty.

I brushed my fingers over the puffy green moss and the cool rocks nearby. Tiny fishes swam in the crystal clear ponds of water at my feet, nibbling energetically at my skin. The water, the air, the whole environment was invigorating. I felt young and strong again, especially knowing my goal was within reach, maybe even by tomorrow. My zest for life and living was again restored. To just be alive at this moment was enough!

* * * * *

The tension felt earlier in the journey was no longer so great. It was still there, but to a much lesser degree; it was almost as if it was caused by my capacity to adjust or not adjust to the jungle and the ways of nature. Is there some meaningfulness to it all?

* * * * *

Thank you, Jack Kerouac.

As all good things must end, so did the shower by the mountain waterfall in the afternoon sun. With regret, I stepped out of the falling water, dressed, and followed the men up the hill to the trail. Soon we were once again chugging our way over the mountainous trail.

With less than an hour of daylight remaining, I sensed the Colombians were quickening their pace. We were now walking even faster than before, and I didn't understand why. I had already been struggling over the increasingly rugged terrain trying to keep their backs within view. They never looked back.

We scaled sharp perpendicular ridges, using our hands, feet and elbows to push and pull our bodies to the top. With every ridge scaled, it was necessary to descend down the opposite side. Usually we slid on our haunches and feet, which proved the quickest and safest way of getting to the bottom. Some portions of the trail would have been impossible for even a mule.

Remember the motorcycle? That seemed such a long time ago. Anyway, it would have been a lost cause on this terrain!

My lack of speed going uphill was overcome by my quickness on the downhill slopes; being able to slide faster on the tough, knob-soled boots. Sliding down the loose gravel was like a fun game, while the Colombians struggled in their soft plastic shoes.

This method of sliding downhill almost proved to be my downfall.

We were walking, or nearly sliding down a trail with a sharp curve to the right. It was late in the day and I was very tired, almost exhausted. Pablo and Tomo were able to negotiate the curve successfully, but in the dim light I failed to see the sharp turn until it was too late and slid down the hill on the soles of my boots past the trail. I was only a few yards from the two men and the trail, but my momentum and the steepness of the hill caused me to lose control. Suddenly I began to roll and tumble. The saddle-bags flapped wildly in the air slapping me about the head and jabbing at my ribs. Sharp rocks and broken branches tore at my skin and clothing as I groped desperately in the air for anything to stop my fall.

Then my left booted foot wedged solidly between two protruding tree roots while the rest of my body continued to roll; then I stopped completely. A sharp, jolting pain shot from my knee and I screamed. The scream didn't ease the pain, but it did attract the attention of my traveling companions. My left leg was bent at the knee and twisted at an odd angle. I sat there staring at it for a long moment, as the nerve under my right eyelid jumped involuntarily. I flinched trying to stop it. Through my distorted and jumpy vision, I could see the knee was not broken, but stretched taunt to the point of tearing.

A few seconds to calm my emotions and I straightened my upper body and thigh to be in line with the twisted knee, but I was still unable to free my foot from the root. The pain, though less sharp, remained. Pablo and Tomo slid down the stony slope to help; both laughed when they saw that I was essentially okay.

They helped pull the booted foot from the wedging roots and pulled me upright. Supported by them and my right leg, I tested the strained knee; flexing and shaking it several times. Fortunately, no bones were broken or ligaments damaged; it was only a minor sprain.

Another day of luck!

In a short while, I was gingerly making my way down the trail, and, after a short distance, my Colombian friends decided to call it a day and make camp. Using our machetes, we unburdened ourselves of the heavy gear and each cleared an area for hammocks; mine a comfortable ten yards from theirs.

Before trying to sleep, I was lured to the tall blazing fire Pablo & Tomo had built. It was huge and had flames leaping high to burn the over-hanging leaves and branches above. But the heat offered dryness to my clothing, warmth to my shivering body, and comfort to my swollen knee. I was surprised, almost shocked, to see in the fire's light the two Colombians sleeping together *in one hammock*! How two grown men were able to sleep in one hammock, albeit larger than mine, was perplexing. Actually, the mere idea of sleeping every night for a lifetime in a hammock was foreign.

Returning to my hammock in the hope of some good sleep, I allowed myself a chuckle at *them* for a change when noticing each man had to sleep with their feet near the nose of the other.

*   *   *   *   *

It was now the morning of March 16, 1965.

Predictably, I awoke with a sore, stiff knee and a mind dulled by lack of sound sleep, but doubly determined to reach the sovereign territory of Colombia. Hurriedly tearing my well-worn jacket into long narrow strips of cloth for an "ace" bandage, I was soon returned to the trail.

After less than an hour of limping along the trail in a north easterly direction, the knee became less and less of a distraction, and I came to know why the Colombians had pushed so hard during the last hours of yesterdays walking. We came to an acre of open land on the top of the highest mountain range when Pablo said:

"En Colombia, ahora!"

It took some time for those words to translate and sink into my comprehension; like "WOW", at last!!! In front of me was Colombia and all of South America. Behind me were the Darien Jungle, Central America and North America. I was on the threshold of what had been an elusive, tormented, hopeful and glorious drawn-out dream conceived in California. It seemed so long ago, through many resurrections.

There were no walls, fences, or barbed wire here; there was nothing to indicate a boundary between two countries. There was, however, one man-made marker. It was an eight foot tall *obelisk* standing lonely and bravely in the center of the clearing in recognition of separation.

This was _my_ idea of a border. If only all the borders in all the world could be like this one.

It was carved out of blue-grey marble and easily weighed five hundred pounds or more. I had difficulty imagining how the government officials of the two nations were able to come together and place this obelisk on top of a mountain in the middle of nowhere; it had probably been done by a helicopter. On two of the four sides, the ones facing each country, was a single simple brass ornament engraved with the numerical data of its location on the map: the latitude, longitude, hours, minutes, and seconds. After a moment's hesitation, I realized I didn't have to prove to anybody what I had done. I did it, I knew I had done it, and that was all that was necessary. I had made it through the Darien Jungle. I was in South America.

I remember having the thought of wanting to write down the engraved numbers, but didn't. I was much too overwhelmed with the emotions and with the richness of the moment to write anything.

I sat on the ground resting my back and elbows on the high smooth base of the obelisk, and felt a great gush of weariness flow out of my depleted body, mind, and soul; like an athlete at the end of a game. I had made it! I had reached my goal, achieved my dream, and fulfilled my longings of *becoming*. Exactly what I was becoming I didn't know. But I did know I had become a better person and a truer man. It was a moment in time when I had become *more*, more than what I was at the start of this cruise. Words became meaningless. The shakedown cruise was successful!

The experience was real, and that's what counted. It became an everlasting possession layered upon all previous experiences, and an ingredient for the uniqueness of identity. Simultaneously, I was awakening latent potentials. Ah, the hoped-for more and better experiences to come; experiences, experiences, and more experiences. Would this provide meaningfulness? Is the wisdom of experience ripened by time?

I was light-headed and giddy with joy. I wanted to yell and scream to share the moment with everyone, but only Pablo and Tomo were there; civilization was still a long way off.

But for now, the top of the mountain was gaily lit by the early sunlight illuminating our faces and the top of the mountain. And even though the area was littered with fallen and partially fallen trees, several old lean-to shelters, and rusted tin cans, it still looked beautiful.

I wanted to do something momentous, something spectacular, but didn't. Instead, Pablo, Tomo, and I sat in a circle for some food and water. After rummaging through the saddle-bags, I opened the last can of C-Rations (delicious pork and beans) and shared a small piece of hard bread from Pinogana.

We smoked cigarettes and tried to talk about things important in our lives. It felt as if the two Colombians at last accepted me as more than a soft foreigner, viewing me as a near-equal in perseverance and stamina; it was as if I were one of them.

After a brief rest, we agreed it best to start walking again. They said we would be at the first outpost of Colombian civilization by sunset; but we were still many hours away.

* * * * *

The eight hours immediately following our departure from the obelisk on the top of the mountain at the borders were filled with the always adventurous task of walking *down*, down the mountains; but still in a north easterly direction. I was never able to establish in my mind which was the more grueling: the grunt of uphill climbing or the stumbling of downhill hiking.

My strained knee constantly buckled under my upper body weight often causing me to fall to the ground; my thighs burnt from the friction of muscle movement; my shoulders ached from the saddle bag straps; my lungs wanted to burst open. But I had become so disciplined and accustomed to pain it was just another part of daily life.

Finally, the mountains and hills began to peter out, and I was about to make an exit from the Darien Jungle; the organic refuge that had been my home and constant companion for so long. But the end did not come as suddenly as it began. Rather, it was ever so gradual and subtle.

I began to notice the jungle disappearing at the first sign of human life in a quaint Indian village (Arquia?) as we came out of the foothills. The sun was only an hour short of disappearing. A quiet stream rippled past the huts, and we all sat down and cooled our hot and sweaty feet in the few inches of chilled mountain water. Knee still swollen, I dampened the rags that acted like an "ace" bandage to reduce swelling.

After just a few minutes of this relief, we were approached by several Indians, all of whom, apparently, knew Pablo well. But these were not Cuna, either in dress or physical appearance. Soon other Indians unselfishly offered fresh bananas and bowls of thick *chicha* to drink. We stayed only thirty minutes before continuing down the dirt trail.

The terrain had finally taken a favorable turn, and the trail showed signs of frequent use. The now-widened trail followed through broad groves of banana trees, becoming clearer with each mile of forward progress. It looked like we were on a sprawling and meticulously well-cultivated plantation with nearby acres of sugarcane. Needless to say, we stopped to refresh ourselves with some of the more-ripe bananas and chew on sugar cane and suck out the sweetness.

And again, ever so gradually, the landscape was changing. A new world was opening up. The snarling green jaws of the jungle that had been chewing at me for four weeks had finally let go; opened up. Walking forward, eyes ablaze, nature unveiled the most beautiful portrait of herself that I had seen in a long, long time. It was a velvety-soft pasture of *grass*, breathtakingly wide and wonderfully smooth, stretching fifteen to twenty acres in front of me. What a sight! Its yellow-green grass seemed of the finest texture and perfectly blended gently into the pinkish setting sun.

To most, it was a common-place sight, but to me it represented the first real sign of civilization anywhere; but especially now in South America. I felt ready to breathe deep again and a chance to move freely about.

In the foreground, not fifty feet from where I stood, was a solitary cow. It was just an ordinary cow grazing on the sunlit grass; and picture perfect. A drooping wire fence broke the continuous line of rolling grass hills containing the animal within the pasture. Happiness welled within and my eyes burned from salty tears. Hastily I tried catching up to Pablo and Tomo, already a hundred yards ahead of me. We were in hot pursuit of thin streaks of black smoke rising straight into the air from the conglomeration of buildings two or three miles ahead.

We came to the first village of Colombia. Its name was *Unguia*.

Soon Pablo and Tomo were lost in the crowd of faces in this small frontier town; I would never see them again. Once again, I was left to carve out an existence on my own.

* * * * *

I came to know the town of *Unguia* only too well. Unable to find this village on any map or in any books, I was uncertain of how to spell its name. But the villagers of *Unguia* epitomized, to me, some of the worst of humanity: hatred, greed, illiteracy, immorality. These people lived on the fringe of civilization and abided only by the laws governing survival. Connivance and thievery were their *modus operandi*.

Women sat hunched on decaying wooden floors in their shacks, skirts dangling between their bared knees, smoking cigarettes with the lighted end in their mouths. Half-drunk men gathered in small groups trying to con each other out of cigarettes while talking about the next big opportunity awaiting them if only they could return to Bogotá. Most of them had been there and returned empty-handed. Children were scantily clothed and bore scars of diseases, insect bites, and even machete cuts. There were women there with blankets over their shoulders and Stetson hats on their heads.

In short, it was one of the most undesirable hell-holes I'd ever seen. Yet somehow I loved it! I was attracted to the atmosphere of self-governing, where anything goes without pretense. I loved the strange smells mingled with the aroma of intrigue and excitement. It was what life must have been like a hundred years ago in the old Wild West, Indians and all.

I discovered, not to my surprise, that Pablo and Tomo were, in fact, thieves and smugglers wanted by both the Panamanian and Colombian authorities. And, of course, they only used me to present a degree of legitimacy, but, I used them too.

During my twenty-four hours in *Unguia*, I was robbed, not once, but twice, of what few material possessions I had, including all my sleeping gear. (Not my passport and money. Each was always carried on my body in a small pouch around my neck.) But even this could not dampen the excitement I felt. I would have sold my boots if necessary, just to have the experience of being there.

To get out of *Unguia*, I had to use their only link to the outside world – a riverboat. Each day the overloaded boat would chug its way to Turbo, carrying the maximum of twelve passengers and hundreds of pounds of bananas, sugar cane, and tightly wrapped boxes.

On my day of departure, twelve pulling and pushing people battered and clamored aboard the poorly painted, dinky, former tugboat. A crew of two worked feverishly loading the freight. If the plump, white-bearded captain of the ship had not taken a special interest in me, it would have been impossible to get aboard. I paid him ten American dollars (a large sum) to be the thirteenth passenger.

The boat soon wobbled away from the tiny *Unguia* loading dock as the passengers shuffled themselves into a more permanent resting place for the three or four hour haul to Turbo.

It was a fun trip and reminded me of the "African Queen" movie as it motored along at a snail's pace for the first hour, hardly able to squeeze past the sticky bottom and pressing watery vegetation. Those unfortunate passengers forced near the railings were cursed by the constant slapping of high grass and thick green leaves. The captain navigated his boat through several channels in which no water could be seen; so thick were the floating water lilies and out-growing trees.

Nonetheless, the experienced captain persisted through with determination and confidence as, I'm certain, he must have done a hundred times before. The ship's bow parted the flattened leaves and pushed aside the white lilies without resistance. The propeller sliced the plants into tiny bits, leaving a trail of churning white water mixed with shredded greens. Friendly and brightly colored parrots positioned themselves on nearby trees observing the passing spectacle.

The parrots, water lilies, and overhanging trees along the river were the last sights I ever saw of the Darien Jungle.

*   *   *   *   *

Soon all the appealing, yet intimidating, maze of green was behind me. The engine pushed the boat through the rolling waves of the Golfo de Urabá, as Turbo, only a mile away, began to grow in size. The easily recognizable smell of saltwater from the larger Golfo del Darién and the Atlantic Ocean filled my senses triggering an emotional beckoning as I tried to review the outstanding experiences of the past several months.

Looking up at the white clouds and down at the crystal blue water, I became mesmerized by the bubbly waves breaking over the slippery bow of the over laden boat. Trade winds fluffed my hair to one side filling my lungs with a refreshing cleanness, while my mind regained an increasing fascination with the ocean. There are so many places to go; deserts, mountains, and railway stations - so much to do.

I had passed the test of planning and executing an adventurous experience from beginning to end; from California to Colombia; from North America to South America.

Ah, the tonic of adventure, the lure of curiosity. How I love them both! The dread of monotony will always kick start me on yet another voyage of discovery. I can see an endless career of adventure and a life of anticipation. There will be uncertainties but always will the uncertainties be wedded to security, the security of being on the path and the plethora of experiential truth. Searching for truth, seeing the beauty, sharing the goodness are permanent possessions. The urge for adventure is supreme.

The bustling city of Turbo was before me, within swimming distance if necessary. I allowed myself only the briefest backward glance turned and readied myself for the next adventure.

The shakedown cruise was over.

The End

Epilogue

This could read more like a *travelogue* than an epilogue; so remember to keep breathing.)

It was an easy trip from Turbo to Medellin. But the bus ride to the Colombian capitol, Bogota, over the treacherous Andes Mountain roads was long, cold, and wet – wet only because a fellow passenger next to me fell asleep with his head on my shoulder and slobbered continuously. He was probably a little drunk.

In Bogota I stopped in the American Consulate to inform them of my trek and safe arrival. Essentially, they patted me on the head and said: "Nice little boy. Now why don't you just gather your belongings and return home."

For some unknown reason, I traveled through neighboring Venezuela, stopping in their capitol of Caracas for a short while. I knew it wasn't the place for me when machine gun shots rang out around me. Several bullets buzzed nearby while sitting on a bench in the central park; not once, but twice. The shopkeepers who had befriended me said it happens all the time, and not to worry.

I was running out of money and decided it was time to return to the States by way of island-hopping up the Caribbean. How I traveled from Caracas to Trinidad, the most southern of the Caribbean Islands has long ago escaped my memory. What I do remember is meeting a young English maiden who was traveling to the island of Antigua, several islands up the line. Her name was Carolyn and she was going there to meet a girlfriend and crew on a sailboat for passage to England. Did I want to come along?

Carolyn's best girlfriend was the wife/partner of the captain of this big beautiful sailboat, a 129-foot square-rig schooner named "Panda". The captain was more impressed with the fact that I was a paratrooper than with the little sailing experience I had. He agreed to take me along as one of the crew! Sailing the North Atlantic was an incredible experience full of dangerous high seas, romance, and camaraderie, but much too voluminous to describe in this writing.

(From the internet, I later discovered the sad fate of the "Panda". Nine or ten years after our 1965 crossing she was being refitted off the Caribbean Island of Martinique and was lost to a fire.)

Carolyn and I spent the summer hitchhiking through Europe, then living in a windmill on the island of Formentera, near Ibiza in the Balearic Islands. Carolyn returned to England and I forged my way to the Canary Islands off the West coast of Africa, seeking passage back to the Caribbean and eventually to the US.

Eventually, I became a crew member on a 96-foot steel-hulled ketch named "La Flore", bearing a Swiss flag. Compared to the North Atlantic, sailing the South Atlantic was a dream; we barely changed the sails more than half a dozen times.

In Barbados, the owner moved aboard, and we sailed north, stopped at all the major islands up the Caribbean to the American Virgin Islands. There I met Arlene, the love of my life. She was there with a girlfriend on vacation from Brooklyn College.

Fate forced me into making a life-changing decision when the owner of "La Flore" offered to send me to nautical school in England to get official maritime papers and become his next captain – the current Norwegian captain was soon retiring. The offer created a firestorm of a conflict within me: a life of sailing the high seas *or* to follow my love, wherever it would take us.

Well, the rest is history as they say.

But not quite...

Arlene and I spent the next 4 years living on the beach in Venice, California, while she completed her PhD in psychology at the University of Southern California. In June of 1970, we had a hippy-style wedding with our friends, drove an old Chevy across the US to New York City and had a good Jewish wedding with the families.

Thereafter, we filled our backpacks with most of our worldly possessions, jumped on a Greek freighter and spent the next two years traveling out of the US. After Israel, we traveled overland to India, up to Nepal, and on to Southeast Asia. From there we went down to Bali, Indonesia and made another fateful decision.

It was then, while in a deep soul-searching meditation, and for the first and only time in my life, I heard a voice inside me speak. The voice said: "*A man must do everything.*" Needless to say it left a profound impression on my psyche. Consequently, we signed on as crew on a 40-foot yawl-rig sailboat, named "Wanderer", and sailed 3,600 miles across the Indian Ocean along the equator to the Seychelle Islands, within a thousand miles of the African coast. (Another story?)

After nine glorious months of fun in the sun on these islands, we board a freighter to Pakistan, and then bussed our way to Europe. We paid for two cheap seats on a flight from England to Philadelphia, PA chartered by bird-watchers. After living for a season in Orlando, FL where Arlene taught at Florida Technological University we had yet another adventure.

A group of ten friends and students converted an old school bus into a camper, painted "GOD IS LOVE" across both sides, and drove it to Costa Rica; filled with the optimism of starting our own commune, our own society. After nine months of draining enthusiasm, but having completed our first reading of The Urantia Book, Arlene and I were sitting on a log near the top of a mountain top wondering: "What was next for us?"

We shared our inner longings of a need to settle in our own country and culture, raise a family, and to be of service.

Returning, we moved to Pueblo, Colorado in 1975 and began the most exciting adventure of all; and in the process experienced growing from physical excitements, into intellectual pursuits, and onto our first priority of a personal relationship with God.

We've lived in Pueblo for the past 32 years and carved out a good life in this great community. I received a college degree at the local university and became a clinical therapist at Parkview Hospital and retired after 25 years; Arlene developed a private practice in clinical psychology that she still maintains. We co-created a family and raised Jonathan, Matthew, and Adam to adulthood.

We still love to travel and read The Urantia Book, and have broadened our adventure horizons to include the intellectual and the spiritual.

*   *   *   *   *

So, there it is! Now you know my whole life.
Well...almost.

www.ingramcontent.com/pod-product-compliance
Lightning Source LLC
Chambersburg PA
CBHW031831090426
42741CB00005B/200